AF324916

In *Human Origins and Evolution in a Malthusian Economy*, Angus
C. Chu offers a brilliant synthesis of economic growth theory and evolutionary biology, establishing a dynamic framework that extends
unified growth theory into the realm of human evolutionary processes. This insightful work navigates the complex interplay between
biological adaptations and economic forces, from the earliest days of
the *Homo* species to the intricacies of modern economies.

By integrating a Malthusian growth framework with pivotal
moments in human history, such as the Neolithic and Industrial Revolutions, Chu provides a fresh perspective on the fundamental economic drivers of human evolution. His analysis broadens the scope of
evolutionary economics and deepens our understanding of how these
economic mechanisms have shaped human societies across millennia.

Chu's narrative is a compelling invitation to reevaluate conventional economic theories, highlighting the role of natural selection and
economic principles in shaping our past and influencing our future.
This book is a must-read for anyone interested in the intersections of
economics, history, and biology and stands as a significant contribution to the literature. It promises to captivate economists, historians,
and biologists alike, inspiring ongoing discussion and research into
the economic behaviours that drive human evolution and societal
development.

Guido Cozzi
University of St. Gallen

An intriguing and thought-provoking theoretical perspective on the
evolution of the human species, shedding light on the emergence of
our species and its transformative journey over the course of history.

Oded Galor
Brown University and author of
The Journey of Humanity

An extraordinary synthesis of evolutionary biology and economic theory, Angus C. Chu's *Human Origins and Evolution in a Malthusian Economy* offers a groundbreaking perspective on humanity's journey from prehistoric hunter-gatherers to industrialized societies. Through a sophisticated growth-theoretic lens, Chu masterfully unpacks the critical transitions that define human history, from brain evolution and migration to agricultural and industrial revolutions. This book is essential reading for anyone seeking to understand the economic forces that have shaped—and continue to shape—our species.

Aditya Goenka
University of Birmingham

Angus Chu brilliantly fleshes out the core of human development from the hunter-gatherer era through to the Neolithic Revolution, which eventuated into the Industrial Revolution and the modern growth regime. This is achieved without resorting to long complicated derivations and involved discussions. The chapters are short and clear, with sharp introductions and conclusions, and human development is analysed in chronological order through economic development. The book is an excellent resource for courses in economic growth that need a short introduction to the essence of economic development before moving onto unified growth models of the fertility transition and neoclassical and endogenous growth models. The book will also have general appeal to non-specialist students and academics who are interested in human accomplishment in the ultra-long run.

Jakob Madsen
University of Western Australia

This is an outstanding account of the evolution of human life and the livelihood transition from a traditional agricultural society to a modern industrial economy—a highly readable and easily accessible book containing cutting-edge macroeconomic tools. It is essential reading for those with an interest in the issues of the historical evolution of human society and factors explaining its development. Employing state-of-the-art modelling approaches, this advanced book offers a blend of analytical, quantitative and evolutionary insights about the origins of contemporary economic growth and development across different eras.

Sushanta Mallick
Queen Mary University of London

A pioneering exploration of human evolution through the lens of economic theory. This book offers innovative perspectives on human evolution and population dynamics, making it a must-read for anyone at the crossroads of economics, evolutionary biology and paleoanthropology.

Sasha Talavera
University of Birmingham

Human Origins and Evolution in a Malthusian Economy

Human Origins and Evolution in a Malthusian Economy

Angus C. Chu

University of Macau, Macau, China

Foreword by
Pietro F. Peretto

World Scientific

EW JERSEY · LONDON · SINGAPORE · BEIJING · SHANGHAI · HONG KONG · TAIPEI · CHENNAI · TOKYO

Published by

World Scientific Publishing Europe Ltd.

57 Shelton Street, Covent Garden, London WC2H 9HE

Head office: 5 Toh Tuck Link, Singapore 596224

USA office: 27 Warren Street, Suite 401-402, Hackensack, NJ 07601

Library of Congress Control Number: 2025015481

British Library Cataloguing-in-Publication Data
A catalogue record for this book is available from the British Library.

HUMAN ORIGINS AND EVOLUTION IN A MALTHUSIAN ECONOMY

ISBN 978-1-80061-734-6 (hardcover)
ISBN 978-1-80061-735-3 (ebook for institutions)
ISBN 978-1-80061-736-0 (ebook for individuals)

For any available supplementary material, please visit
https://www.worldscientific.com/worldscibooks/10.1142/Q0510#t=suppl

Desk Editors: Nambirajan Karuppiah/Gabriel Rawlinson

Typeset by Stallion Press
Email: enquiries@stallionpress.com

This book is dedicated to Erica. May she rest in peace.

Foreword

Angus Chu has spent his entire career thinking and writing about economic growth. The driving force behind this focus is the belief that economic growth is good and that societies should cherish and pursue it. While the cherishing is straightforward and perhaps easy, the pursuing is hard; it requires an understanding of the mechanisms that drive it, particularly an understanding that permits the formulation of intelligent and effective policies to support it and the intelligent and effective design of institutions that allow its flourishing in the first place. Such understanding arises from good theory—theory that rests on solid conceptual foundations and is then expressed in rigorous mathematical language. Most importantly, theory that is firmly grounded in real-world facts and validated through robust empirical testing. This is the kind of theory that Angus has produced throughout a career dedicated to studying, researching, and teaching economics.

Why is economic growth good? Just a few years ago, the question would not even be asked in economics. Indeed, economists like Angus, who were trained and then joined the profession in the 1990s, probably had not heard it. Society and economics simply thought it was self-evident that more resources available for human use are a good thing. With more resources available, society can educate children, provide for the weak and needy, build hospitals, roads, bridges, and schools, train the next generation of scientists, engineers, doctors, and all sorts of skilled individuals who build upon past achievements to further improve the human condition. A key component of this process involves the development of ideas that allow society to design and build institutions to enable, encourage, and support the pursuit of the new, the exploration of the different, and the questioning of the status quo, or, in other words, the institutions that nurture the quest for new ideas building upon existing ones.

Angus has spent his intellectual career contributing to the collective process of questioning the existing understanding of economic growth in pursuit of original, novel, and useful insights that add to the stock of knowledge and, brick by brick, built the magnificent edifice that is modern growth theory. He has participated in the enterprise of writing and publishing dozens of articles and several books. His research spans multiple areas of growth economics, reflecting his innate curiosity and versatility.

This book further expands the range of Angus's contributions. It develops a simple and yet insightful economic theory of the origins and evolution of humanity throughout the Malthusian epoch, which ended only a couple of centuries ago with the Industrial Revolution, and beyond. It thus covers the bulk of the human experience and offers some illuminating thoughts about the future. This is an area of research that developed quite recently—it really took off in the early 2000s—but has already produced an avalanche of new insights and a novel understanding of the process of economic growth broadly construed and of the forces that drive it. With this book, Angus claims his rightful place as one of the principal contributors to the development of the field.

It has been my privilege to spend my own career—we are roughly contemporaries—in the company of a person like Angus, first from a distance, reading his research, and then meeting him in person and developing a gratifying and productive collaboration. Most of all,

I am grateful that we became friends. I look forward to many more years of joint work on novel and exciting ideas.

Pietro Peretto
Durham, NC
February 4, 2025

Preface

This book develops an economic theory of the entirety of human evolution. Early members of our genus *Homo* emerged over 2 million years ago. Then, they gradually evolved into *Homo sapiens* about 300,000 years ago. During most of their existence, early modern humans were hunter-gatherers and shared this planet with archaic humans, such as Neanderthals and Denisovans. So, how did *Homo sapiens* emerge? Why did other human species become extinct but early modern humans survive? Why do modern humans still carry DNA from archaic humans? What caused the transition of human society from hunting-gathering tribes to agricultural settlements and the subsequent transition from an agricultural economy to an industrial economy? And how has education affected the emergence of innovation and given rise to the transition from pre-industrial stagnation to economic growth in modern times? This book develops a growth-theoretic framework that can be used to explore the origins of human species and the evolution of human society across different stages.

Chapter 1 presents a canonical Malthusian growth model, which will be extended in subsequent chapters to incorporate different elements for exploring the above questions. Chapter 2 applies the Malthusian growth model to explore the biological evolution of human brain size. Chapter 3 introduces multiple regions to the

Malthusian growth model to explore the causes and consequences of prehistoric human migration. Chapter 4 explores the extinction of archaic humans and the survival of *Homo sapiens*. This chapter also analyzes the presence of archaic humans' DNA in modern humans. Chapter 5 considers the economic evolution of human society from hunting-gathering tribes to agricultural settlements (i.e., the Neolithic Revolution). Chapter 6 explores the political evolution of an agricultural society from multiple competing states to a unified empire. Chapter 7 considers the economic evolution of human society from an agricultural economy to an industrial economy (i.e., the Industrial Revolution). Chapter 8 introduces a market structure of monopolistic competition and explores its implications on the industrialization of the economy. Chapter 9 examines the importance of education in the emergence of innovation and technological progress in a post-industrial economy. Chapter 10 explores the potential impact of evolutionary processes on innovation and technological progress in modern times.

About the Author

Angus C. Chu was born in Hong Kong and studied at Simon Fraser University and the University of British Columbia in Canada. He obtained his PhD in economics from the University of Michigan. He is currently a distinguished professor and the head of the Department of Economics at the University of Macau. He was the chair of macroeconomics at the University of Liverpool. Before that, he served as the professor of economics at Fudan University. His research focuses on macroeconomics, economic growth, innovation, and intellectual property rights. His recent research relates to evolutionary economics, focusing on the evolution of human society. His research has appeared in journals such as the *European Economic Review, International Economic Review, Journal of Development Economics, Journal of Economic Growth, Journal of International Economics, Journal of Money, Credit and Banking, Journal of Population Economics, Journal of Urban Economics*, and *Review of Economic Dynamics*. His textbook *Advanced Macroeconomics: An Introduction for Undergraduates* was published by World Scientific in 2020. Its Chinese adaptation, *Introduction to Advanced Macroeconomics* (with Xilin Wang), was published by Tsinghua University Press in 2021. According to IDEAS/RePEc Rankings, he is among the top 5% of economists in the world and also among the top 30, top 50, and top 80 economists in the fields of intellectual property rights, economic growth, and innovation, respectively. He currently serves as a co-editor-in-chief for *Economic Modelling*.

Acknowledgements

I am most grateful to Amanda, Alvin, and Alice. I could not have undertaken this journey without their loving support. I would also like to thank my co-authors, Guido Cozzi, Haichao Fan, Yuichi Furukawa, Zonglai Kou, Pietro Peretto, Xilin Wang, and Rongxin Xu for their invaluable contributions to our research agenda that forms the basis of this book. Last but not least, I would like to thank Oded Galor for his insightful comments and for being an inspiration.

Contents

Part I
Prehistoric Era

Chapter 1

Hunting-Gathering in a Malthusian Economy

In this book, we develop a growth-theoretic framework based on the Malthusian growth model to explore the evolution of human society. The Malthusian growth model is based on the influential work of Malthus (1798), who observed that population growth is limited by the availability of natural resources.[1] In this chapter, we present a modern canonical version of the Malthusian growth model, which serves as our baseline model to be extended in subsequent chapters.[2]

The Malthusian growth model features endogenous fertility, which is increasing in the level of food output per capita. Given that food production is subject to decreasing returns to scale in labor, a larger population size reduces the level of food output per capita. Therefore, as the population size increases, the population growth rate decreases and eventually converges to zero. The main insight we obtain from this growth-theoretic framework is that the population growth rate is determined by the endogenous fertility decision of utility-maximizing agents and influenced by the following determinants: productivity in food production, labor supply, the

---

[1] See Ehrlich and Lui (1997) for a review of the literature.

[2] See also Ashraf and Galor (2011) for an elegant treatment of the Malthusian model.

amount of land, fertility preference, and fertility cost. Furthermore, the population size converges to a steady-state level, which is decreasing in the fertility cost but increasing in the degree of fertility preference, the level of productivity, the supply of labor, and the amount of land. However, the long-run level of food output per capita depends only on the fertility cost and the degree of fertility preference but not on the level of productivity, the supply of labor, or the amount of land. This finding captures the essence of a Malthusian trap, in which technological advances do not improve the standard of living in the long run. As Galor (2022, pp. 4–5) writes, "during the period known as the Malthusian epoch [...] the fruits of technological advancements were channelled primarily towards larger and denser populations."

1.1 A Hunting-Gathering Malthusian Growth Model

This section presents a simple Malthusian growth model of hunting-gathering.[3] Consider a group of humans, who may be *Homo sapiens* or any archaic humans, such as Neanderthals or Denisovans. The group engages in food production in the form of hunting-gathering within a fixed area of land Z.

1.1.1 Endogenous fertility

There are N_t adult agents at time t. We consider overlapping generations of agents. Each agent lives for two periods. Each adult agent at time t has the following utility function:

$$u_t = (1 - \gamma) \ln c_t + \gamma \ln n_t, \tag{1.1}$$

where the parameter $\gamma \in (0, 1)$ measures the preference for fertility (relative to consumption). n_t is the agent's number of children, who then become adults in the next period. Raising children is costly, and

---

[3] An agricultural Malthusian growth model would yield similar implications to a Malthusian trap in the long run due to the decreasing returns to scale in labor in agricultural production; see Chapter 5.

the level of consumption c_t net of the fertility cost is given by

$$c_t = y_t - \rho n_t, \tag{1.2}$$

where the parameter $\rho > 0$ determines the cost of fertility and y_t is the per capita output of food production.

Substituting (1.2) into (1.1), we derive the utility-maximizing level of fertility as

$$n_t = \frac{\gamma}{\rho} y_t, \tag{1.3}$$

which is increasing in food output y_t and fertility preference γ but decreasing in fertility cost ρ. The utility-maximizing level of consumption is $c_t = (1 - \gamma)y_t$. Each adult agent has n_t children, and the number of adult agents at time t is N_t. Therefore, the law of motion for the adult population size is

$$N_{t+1} = n_t N_t = \frac{\gamma}{\rho} y_t N_t, \tag{1.4}$$

and the growth rate of N_t at time t is

$$\frac{\Delta N_t}{N_t} \equiv \frac{N_{t+1} - N_t}{N_t} = \frac{\gamma}{\rho} y_t - 1, \tag{1.5}$$

which will be referred to simply as the population growth rate.

1.1.2 Hunting-gathering

Total food production from hunting-gathering is given by

$$Y_t = \theta (l N_t)^\alpha Z^{1-\alpha}, \tag{1.6}$$

where $l N_t$ and Z are, respectively, the total amount of labor and land devoted to hunting-gathering. Individual labor supply $l > 0$ is exogenous. The parameters $\theta > 0$ and $\alpha \in (0, 1)$ measure, respectively, the productivity and labor intensity of the hunting-gathering process. Each agent receives y_t units of food output, given by

$$y_t \equiv \frac{Y_t}{N_t} = \frac{\theta (l N_t)^\alpha Z^{1-\alpha}}{N_t} = \theta l^\alpha \left(\frac{Z}{N_t} \right)^{1-\alpha}, \tag{1.7}$$

which is increasing in hunting-gathering productivity θ, labor supply l, and the amount of land Z but decreasing in the population size

N_t due to the decreasing returns to scale (i.e., $\alpha < 1$) in hunting-gathering labor.

1.2   Population Dynamics and the Malthusian Trap

Given an initial level of population N_0 at time 0, we can substitute (1.7) into (1.5) to derive the population growth rate at any time t as

$$\frac{\Delta N_t}{N_t} = \frac{\gamma}{\rho}\theta l^{\alpha}\left(\frac{Z}{N_t}\right)^{1-\alpha} - 1, \tag{1.8}$$

which is increasing in fertility preference γ, hunting-gathering productivity θ, labor supply l, and the amount of land Z but decreasing in fertility cost ρ and the population size N_t at time t. The positive effect of land per capita Z/N_t on population growth captures Malthus's insight that population growth is limited by the amount of natural resources per capita.

Because the population growth rate $\Delta N_t/N_t$ in (1.8) is decreasing in the population level N_t, the dynamics of N_t is globally stable, as shown in Figure 1.1.[4] Therefore, given any initial population level N_0, the population size N_t converges to a unique and stable steady

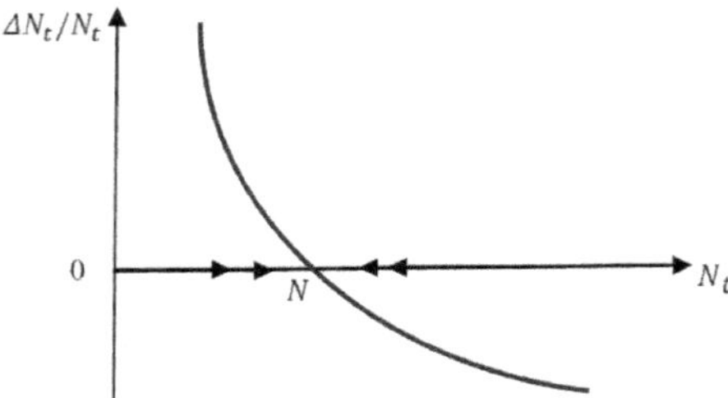

Figure 1.1.   Phase diagram for the population size.

---

[4]Technically, we have a discrete-time dynamic system, but we approximate it with continuous time for simplicity.

state:

$$N = \left(\frac{\gamma}{\rho}\theta l^\alpha\right)^{1/(1-\alpha)} Z, \tag{1.9}$$

which is decreasing in fertility cost ρ but increasing in fertility preference γ, hunting-gathering productivity θ, labor supply l, and the amount of land Z. The positive effects of hunting-gathering productivity θ, labor supply l, and land Z on the population size capture the Malthusian mechanism that higher food production gives rise to a larger population. An additional insight we obtain from the microfoundation of this Malthusian growth model is that fertility preference also matters and has important implications, as we will show.

Imposing $\Delta N_t = 0$ on (1.5) yields the long-run level of food output per capita, given by

$$y = \frac{\rho}{\gamma}, \tag{1.10}$$

and the long-run level of consumption per capita, given by

$$c = (1 - \gamma)y = \frac{\rho(1 - \gamma)}{\gamma}, \tag{1.11}$$

which are both independent of hunting-gathering productivity θ, labor supply l, and land Z, capturing the essence of a Malthusian trap in which higher food production does not improve the standard of living in the long run. However, an increase in fertility cost ρ or a decrease in fertility preference γ would raise the long-run levels of food output and consumption per capita due to their negative effects on the population size and the decreasing returns to scale in food production. In other words, in a Malthusian economy, if agents choose to have fewer offspring, they would enjoy a higher standard of living. However, as we will show in subsequent chapters, choosing to have fewer offspring may give rise to the extinction of their species (or the collapse of their state) when competing with another human species (or another state) and the delay (or even absence) of the Neolithic and Industrial Revolutions.

1.3   Summary and Discussion

In this chapter, we have presented a canonical Malthusian growth model and derived the endogenous population growth rate. This growth-theoretic analysis shows that population growth is determined by the level of productivity in food production, the supply of labor, the amount of land, the degree of fertility preference, and the cost of fertility. Furthermore, the population size converges to a steady-state level, which is decreasing in fertility cost but increasing in fertility preference, the amount of land, labor supply, and productivity in food production. However, the amount of land, labor supply, and productivity in food production have no effect on the steady-state levels of output and consumption per capita because the population is in a Malthusian trap in the long run. Ashraf and Galor (2011) use historical data from the period 1–1500 BC to provide empirical support for some of these theoretical predictions of the Malthusian growth model. Specifically, they find that higher land productivity increased population density but did not affect the standard of living for the one-and-a-half millennia. In subsequent chapters, we extend this baseline Malthusian growth model to explore different aspects of human evolution.

Chapter 2

Human Brain Size Evolution

Archeological evidence shows that there were about a dozen human species in the past. They exhibited morphological differences, especially different brain sizes. The earliest members of our genus *Homo* emerged over 2 million years ago. Since then, the volume of the human brain has gradually increased as humans evolved.[1] *Homo habilis*, who is possibly the earliest known member of our genus and lived from roughly 2.8 million to 1.65 million years ago in Africa according to existing fossil evidence, had a brain size of about 550–690 cm^3.[2] *Homo erectus*, who lived from roughly 2 million to 110,000 years ago in Africa, Asia, and Europe, had a brain size of about 600–1250 cm^3.[3] *Homo heidelbergensis*, who lived from roughly 600,000 to 200,000 years ago in Africa and Europe, had a brain size of about 1100–1400 cm^3. *Homo neanderthalensis*, who is commonly known as the Neanderthals and lived mainly in Europe from possibly 430,000

---

[1] DeSilva *et al.* (2021) find that after a rising trend in human brain size for about 2 million years, there may have been a brain size reduction since 3,000 years ago. A subsequent study by Villmoare and Grabowski (2022) questions the validity of this recent brain size reduction.

[2] There is a debate on whether *Homo habilis* belongs to the genus *Homo*. For example, Wood and Collard (1999) argue that *Homo habilis* should be moved to the genus *Australopithecus*.

[3] It is possible that *Homo erectus* emerged in Asia; see, e.g., Wood (2011) for a discussion.

9

to 40,000 years ago, had a brain size of about 1200–1750 cm^3. *Homo sapiens*, who emerged as early as 300,000 years ago,[4] has an average brain size of about 1400 cm^3. Therefore, except for the Neanderthals who had an even larger brain size than *Homo sapiens*, the human brain size has been increasing from early members of genus *Homo* to modern humans.[5]

This chapter extends the baseline Malthusian growth model in the previous chapter to explore the evolution of human brain size driven by natural selection.[6] A larger brain size has two effects. First, it requires a higher level of consumption due to its metabolic costs. Second, it gives rise to a cognitive advantage and improves hunting-gathering productivity. The first effect represents an evolutionary disadvantage of a larger brain size, whereas the second effect represents its evolutionary advantage.

Within this growth-theoretic framework, we obtain the following insights. First, if the cognitive advantage of a larger brain dominates its higher metabolic costs, then a larger brain size has an overall evolutionary advantage. In this case, the average brain size in the human population increases over time, which is consistent with the rising trend in human brain size that started over 2 million years ago. Second, an improvement in hunting-gathering productivity gives rise to a larger optimal brain size in human evolution. Third, as the average brain size increases, the average level of hunting-gathering productivity also rises, generating a positive feedback loop. As Galor (2022, pp. 13–14) writes, "archaic and early modern humans slowly

---

[4]See Hublin *et al.* (2017) and Richter *et al.* (2017).

[5]Another exception is *Homo floresiensis*, who lived from roughly 190,000 to 50,000 years ago on the island of Flores, Indonesia, and had a brain size of about 420 cm^3; however, this small brain size was likely due to island dwarfism.

[6]This chapter is based on Chu (2024a). See Galor and Moav (2002) for a seminal study on natural selection in the Malthusian economy and also Lagerlof (2007), Galor and Michalopoulos (2012), Collins *et al.* (2014), Dalgaard and Strulik (2015), Galor and Ozak (2016), and Galor and Klemp (2019) for subsequent studies. A recent study by Galor and Savitskiy (2022) explores the evolutionary origins of loss aversion and how they are affected by climatic shocks.

but steadily acquired new skills, mastered the use of fire, developed increasingly sophisticated blades, handaxes, and flint and limestone tools, and created artworks. A key driver of these cultural and technological advancements, which came to define humankind and set us apart from other species, was the evolution of the human brain."

2.1 A Malthusian Model with Human Brain Evolution

We now introduce the evolution of human brain size driven by natural selection to the Malthusian growth model. Specifically, within the human population, there is a large number of families indexed by subscript $i \in \{1, \ldots, m\}$. The families differ in their brain size $b_i \in [b^{\min}, b^{\max}]$, where b_i follows a general distribution across families within the lower bound $b^{\min}$ and upper bound $b^{\max}$ on brain size. Each family i has $N_{i,t}$ adults at time t. Therefore, the total (adult) population size at time t is

$$N_t = \sum_{i=1}^{m} N_{i,t}. \tag{2.1}$$

2.1.1 Metabolic costs of the human brain

Given the metabolic costs of the human brain,[7] a family with a larger brain size b_i requires a higher level of consumption per capita. Therefore, we modify the utility function in (1.1) as follows:

$$u_{i,t} = \beta_i \ln c_{i,t} + \gamma_i \ln n_{i,t}, \tag{2.2}$$

in which the degree of consumption preference $\beta_i = \beta(b_i)$ is assumed to be increasing in brain size b_i, whereas γ_i is the degree of fertility preference. Given the constraint $c_{i,t} = y_{i,t} - \rho n_{i,t}$, the utility-maximizing level of consumption is given by

$$c_{i,t} = \frac{\beta_i}{\beta_i + \gamma_i} y_{i,t}, \tag{2.3}$$

---

[7]See Gonzalez-Forero and Gardner (2018) for estimates of these metabolic costs.

and the utility-maximizing level of fertility is given by

$$n_{i,t} = \frac{\gamma_i}{\beta_i + \gamma_i} \frac{y_{i,t}}{\rho}, \tag{2.4}$$

where fertility cost ρ is assumed to be identical across families for simplicity. Equations (2.3) and (2.4) show that a family with a larger brain size b_i allocates a larger share of food output $y_{i,t}$ to consumption (via a larger β_i) at the expense of fertility.[8] Therefore, if a larger brain size does not carry a cognitive advantage, then families with larger brains would have an evolutionary disadvantage. For notational convenience, we normalize the degree of consumption preference to $\beta_i = 1 - \gamma_i$ and now assume $\gamma_i = \gamma(b_i)$ to be decreasing in brain size b_i.[9]

2.1.2   Cognitive advantage of a larger human brain

To capture the cognitive advantage of a larger human brain,[10] we modify the food production function in (1.6) as follows:

$$Y_{i,t} = \theta_i (l N_{i,t})^\alpha (Z_{i,t})^{1-\alpha}, \tag{2.5}$$

where the level of hunting-gathering productivity $\theta_i = \theta(b_i)$ is assumed to be increasing in brain size b_i due to the cognitive advantage of a larger human brain. Individual labor supply l is exogenous as before and identical across families for simplicity. The amount of land $Z_{i,t}$ utilized by family i for hunting-gathering is assumed to be

---

[8]Chu (2024a) considers a more microfounded approach (in which there is a subsistence consumption requirement that is increasing in brain size b_i) and obtains the same implication that a larger brain size increases consumption at the expense of fertility, but the dynamics of the model becomes more complicated.

[9]Even if we were to specify $u_{i,t} = \beta_i \ln c_{i,t} + \gamma \ln n_{i,t}$ and assume γ to be identical across families, the term in (2.4) would become $\gamma/(\beta_i + \gamma)$, which is still decreasing in the family's brain size b_i via consumption preference β_i.

[10]See van Valen (1974) and Lynn (1990) for estimates of the cognitive advantage of a larger human brain size.

proportional to its population share $s_{i,t} \equiv N_{i,t}/N_t$, such that

$$Z_{i,t} = s_{i,t}Z = \frac{N_{i,t}}{N_t}Z, \tag{2.6}$$

where Z is the total amount of land. Substituting (2.6) into (2.5) yields the level of food output per capita in family i, given by

$$y_{i,t} \equiv \frac{Y_{i,t}}{N_{i,t}} = \frac{\theta_i(lN_{i,t})^\alpha (Z_{i,t})^{1-\alpha}}{N_{i,t}} = \theta_i l^\alpha \left(\frac{Z}{N_t}\right)^{1-\alpha}, \tag{2.7}$$

which is increasing in the level of hunting-gathering productivity $\theta_i = \theta(b_i)$ and the brain size b_i of family i.

2.2 Natural Selection and Brain Size Evolution

Substituting (2.7) and $\beta_i = 1 - \gamma_i$ into (2.4) yields the population growth rate of family i as

$$\frac{\Delta N_{i,t}}{N_{i,t}} = n_{i,t} - 1 = \gamma_i \theta_i \frac{l^\alpha}{\rho} \left(\frac{Z}{N_t}\right)^{1-\alpha} - 1, \tag{2.8}$$

which is independent of $N_{i,t}$ and increasing in $\gamma_i \theta_i$ (i.e., the product of fertility preference γ_i and hunting-gathering productivity θ_i). Therefore, the families with the largest $\gamma_i \theta_i$ dominate the population in the long run (i.e., their population share $s_{i,t} \to 1$). Recall that both the degree of consumption preference $1 - \gamma(b_i)$ and the level of hunting-gathering productivity $\theta(b_i)$ are increasing in brain size $b_i \in [b^{\min}, b^{\max}]$. Therefore, a larger brain size b_i has a negative effect on fertility preference γ_i and a positive effect on hunting-gathering productivity θ_i.

2.2.1 Scenario 1

If the positive effect of brain size always dominates, i.e., $\gamma_i \theta_i$ is monotonically increasing in b_i such that

$$\frac{\partial \gamma_i \theta_i}{\partial b_i} > 0$$

for all $b_i \in [b^{\min}, b^{\max}]$, then families with a larger brain size would have an evolutionary advantage, i.e., their population share $s_{i,t}$ rises over time. Specifically, families that satisfy the following condition would experience a rise in their population share $s_{i,t}$ at time t:

$$\Delta s_{i,t} > 0 \Leftrightarrow \frac{\Delta N_{i,t}}{N_{i,t}} > \frac{\Delta N_t}{N_t} \Leftrightarrow \gamma_i \theta_i > \sum_{i=1}^{m} s_{i,t} \gamma_i \theta_i.$$

In the long run, families with the largest brain size $b^{\max}$ dominate the population (i.e., $s_{i,t}(b_i = b^{\max}) \to 1$). As a result, the average brain size $b_t \equiv \sum_{i=1}^{m} s_{i,t} b_i$ of the human population would increase over time, as observed in archaic humans. As the average brain size increased, the human population evolved into different human species, whose different brain sizes capture one of the defining features of different archaic human species, as documented at the beginning of this chapter.[11]

2.2.2   Scenario 2

If $\gamma_i \theta_i$ is instead an inverted-U function in brain size b_i, then there exists an optimal brain size $b^* \in (b^{\min}, b^{\max})$ from an evolutionary viewpoint (i.e., $s_{i,t}(b_i = b^*) \to 1$). Interestingly, a brain size b_i that is larger than b^* is not optimal in this case, which is consistent with the demise of the Neanderthals who had a larger brain size than *Homo sapiens*. Suppose $\gamma_i \theta_i$ takes the following functional form:

$$\gamma_i \theta_i = (1 - b_i)(1 + \overline{\theta} b_i), \tag{2.9}$$

where $\overline{\theta} > 1$ is a hunting-gathering productivity parameter. Then, the brain size that maximizes $\gamma_i \theta_i$ is given by $b^* = (\overline{\theta} - 1)/(2\overline{\theta})$, which is increasing in $\overline{\theta}$. Therefore, an increase in the hunting-gathering productivity parameter $\overline{\theta}$ raises the optimal brain size. For example, Ofek (2001, p. 73) argues that "the hunting-gathering feeding

---

[11]Schaefer *et al.* (2021) provide evidence that only 1.5–7% of the human genome is unique to *Homo sapiens* and that this small fraction of the human-specific genome is enriched for genes involved in neural development/function.

ecology [that led to an improvement in the quality and quantity of diet] facilitated a growing brain." Our growth-theoretic analysis shows that an improvement in hunting-gathering productivity $\overline{\theta}$ (e.g., the discovery and control of fire possibly by *Homo erectus* for hunting animals and cooking food)[12] could indeed contribute to a larger optimal brain size b^* in human evolution.[13] In this case, the average human brain size $b_t \equiv \sum_{i=1}^{m} s_{i,t} b_i$ rises toward b^*,[14] and the average level of hunting-gathering productivity $\theta_t \equiv \sum_{i=1}^{m} s_{i,t} \theta(b_i)$ also rises over time.

2.3   Summary and Discussion

In this chapter, we have extended the Malthusian growth model to account for the evolution of the human brain. If the cognitive advantage of a larger brain dominates its higher metabolic costs, then the average brain size of the human population increases over time, which is consistent with the rising trend in brain size of human species; see Chu (2024a) for a quantitative analysis that replicates the trend in hominin brain evolution over the past 10 million years. The underlying natural-selection mechanism for human brain evolution in our Malthusian growth model is ecological in nature and driven by the advantage of a larger brain in hunting-gathering and food production. From a quantitative analysis on the evolution of the human brain, Gonzalez-Forero and Gardner (2018) provide evidence that ecological challenges in "finding, caching or processing food" are indeed the main reasons for the evolution of brain size in our genus *Homo*.[15] In the following chapter, we explore the prehistoric migration of early humans.

---

[12] In Chinese mythology, Suiren is credited as the one who introduced humans in ancient China to the use of wooden fire drills to create fire and use it for cooking.

[13] See also Fonseca-Azevedo and Herculano-Houzel (2012).

[14] Here, we assume that the initial average brain size b_0 is below the optimal brain size b^*.

[15] See Heldstab *et al.* (2022) for a survey of the scientific literature on human brain evolution.

Chapter 3

Prehistoric Human Migration

> As prehistoric humans became ever better hunters and gatherers, their population in the fertile regions of Africa increased significantly, ultimately reducing the living space and natural resources available to each of them. Thus, once climatic conditions permitted, humans started branching out to other continents in search of additional fertile grounds. (Galor 2022, p. 18)

The journey of our genus *Homo* is a story of migration. *Homo habilis* emerged in Africa as early as 2.8 million years ago. Some evidence suggests that *Homo habilis* evolved into *Homo erectus* in Africa, who then migrated out of Africa, whereas some evidence suggests that *Homo habilis* evolved into *Homo erectus* in Asia, who then migrated back into Africa.[1] *Homo sapiens* also undertook multiple waves of migration into and out of Africa.[2] Ni *et al.* (2021) estimate the direction of these "dispersals" and find about 40% of dispersals from Africa and 22% into Africa.[3] These prehistoric migrations of our

---

[1] See Wood (2011) for a discussion.

[2] See Lopez *et al.* (2015) for a review of the evidence.

[3] Therefore, they conclude that "[i]nstead of a unidirectional 'out of Africa' model, a multi-directional 'shuttle dispersal model' is more likely to explain the complex phylogenetic connections among African and Eurasian Homo species/populations."

ancestors shape the world that we live in today.[4] So, an important question arises: Why did prehistoric humans migrate?

To explore the above question, we develop a Malthusian growth model with migration to explore the causes and consequences of prehistoric human migration. Our hunting-gathering Malthusian model features two regions. Whether migration from one region to the other region occurs or not depends on the relative population size, the relative land supply, and the relative hunting-gathering productivity between the two regions. Suppose one region is initially uninhabited. Then, migration from the home region to the uninhabited foreign region gives rise to a larger human population in our Malthusian environment, in which the population size is determined by the productivity and supply of natural resources. As Galor (2022, p. 19) writes, "[prehistoric humans] enjoyed access to new grounds for hunting and gathering and started to multiply more rapidly."

3.1　A Malthusian Model with Human Migration

We extend the canonical Malthusian growth model in Chapter 1 by introducing two geographic regions, i and j. Then, we apply this multi-region Malthusian model to explore prehistoric human migration.

3.1.1　Endogenous fertility

As before, we consider overlapping generations of agents, who live for two periods. The utility function of an adult agent in region i at

---

[4]See Ashraf and Galor (2013) and Ashraf *et al.* (2021) for a comprehensive review of the implications of these prehistoric migrations on human genetic diversity and economic development in modern times. A recent study by Galor *et al.* (2024) explores their interesting implications on the degree of cultural diversity across countries.

time t is

$$u_t^i = (1 - \gamma) \ln c_t^i + \gamma \ln n_t^i, \tag{3.1}$$

where $\gamma \in (0, 1)$ measures preference for fertility n_t^i. The agent's children then become adults in the next period. The cost of raising children is ρn_t^i, where $\rho > 0$ is the cost per child. Both fertility cost and consumption c_t^i are in units of food output y_t^i. The agent's resource constraint is

$$c_t^i + \rho n_t^i = y_t^i. \tag{3.2}$$

We substitute (3.2) into (3.1) to derive the levels of fertility and consumption:

$$n_t^i = \frac{\gamma}{\rho} y_t^i, \tag{3.3}$$

$$c_t^i = (1 - \gamma) y_t^i. \tag{3.4}$$

The number of adult agents in region i at the beginning of time t is N_t^i, but some of these agents M_t^i migrate to the other region j before food production, consumption, and fertility take place. Each remaining adult agent in region i has n_t^i children at the end of time t. Therefore, the law of motion for the number of adult agents in region i is

$$N_{t+1}^i = n_t^i(N_t^i - M_t^i) = \frac{\gamma}{\rho} y_t^i(N_t^i - M_t^i), \tag{3.5}$$

which uses (3.3). We also derive the population growth rate in region i as

$$\frac{\Delta N_t^i}{N_t^i} \equiv \frac{N_{t+1}^i - N_t^i}{N_t^i} = \frac{\gamma}{\rho} y_t^i \left(1 - \frac{M_t^i}{N_t^i}\right) - 1, \tag{3.6}$$

which is increasing in region i's food output y_t^i and the agents' fertility preference γ but decreasing in fertility cost ρ and the level of migration M_t^i.

3.1.2   Hunting-gathering

In region i, the food output of an agent, who devotes l units of labor to hunting-gathering, is

$$y_t^i = \theta^i l^\alpha \left(\frac{Z^i}{N_t^i - M_t^i} \right)^{1-\alpha}, \tag{3.7}$$

where $\theta^i > 0$ measures hunting-gathering productivity in region i. The parameter $\alpha \in (0,1)$ measures labor intensity in hunting-gathering and is the same across regions for simplicity. The supply of land in region i is Z^i, and the land input per agent in the region is $Z^i/(N_t^i - M_t^i)$, where $N_t^i - M_t^i$ is the number of agents who remain in region i at time t.

3.1.3   Migration

Substituting (3.7) into (3.3) and (3.4) yields the levels of fertility and consumption in region i:

$$n_t^i = \frac{\gamma}{\rho} \theta^i l^\alpha \left(\frac{Z^i}{N_t^i - M_t^i} \right)^{1-\alpha}, \tag{3.8}$$

$$c_t^i = (1 - \gamma) \theta^i l^\alpha \left(\frac{Z^i}{N_t^i - M_t^i} \right)^{1-\alpha}. \tag{3.9}$$

Then, substituting (3.8) and (3.9) into (3.1) yields the utility of each agent in region i as

$$u_t^i = (1-\gamma)\ln(1-\gamma) + \gamma\ln\left(\frac{\gamma}{\rho}\right) + \ln\left[\theta^i l^\alpha \left(\frac{Z^i}{N_t^i - M_t^i}\right)^{1-\alpha}\right]. \tag{3.10}$$

Similarly, the utility of each agent in region j is

$$u_t^j = (1-\gamma)\ln(1-\gamma) + \gamma\ln\left(\frac{\gamma}{\rho}\right) + \ln\left[\theta^j l^\alpha \left(\frac{Z^j}{N_t^j + M_t^i}\right)^{1-\alpha}\right], \tag{3.11}$$

where $N_t^j + M_t^i$ is the number of adult agents in region j after the migration from region i to region j takes place at time t.

Given the possibility of migration, agents must be indifferent between residing in the two regions. In other words, the utility of agents in the two regions must be equal such that[5]

$$u_t^i = u_t^j. \qquad (3.12)$$

Substituting (3.10) and (3.11) into (3.12) yields the level of migration at time t as

$$M_t^i = \frac{\Theta^j Z^j}{\Theta^i Z^i + \Theta^j Z^j} N_t^i - \frac{\Theta^i Z^i}{\Theta^i Z^i + \Theta^j Z^j} N_t^j, \qquad (3.13)$$

where the composite parameters are defined as $\Theta^i \equiv (\theta^i)^{1/(1-\alpha)}$ and $\Theta^j \equiv (\theta^j)^{1/(1-\alpha)}$. Given $\{N_t^i, N_t^j\}$, the level of migration M_t^i from region i to region j is decreasing in region i's productivity θ^i and land supply Z^i but increasing in region j's productivity θ^j and land supply Z^j.

Furthermore, (3.13) shows that migration from region i to region j occurs (i.e., $M_t^i > 0$) if and only if

$$M_t^i > 0 \Leftrightarrow \frac{N_t^i}{N_t^j} > \frac{\Theta^i Z^i}{\Theta^j Z^j} \Leftrightarrow \frac{\Theta^j Z^j}{N_t^j} > \frac{\Theta^i Z^i}{N_t^i}, \qquad (3.14)$$

which requires the productivity and supply of natural resources per agent in region j to be greater than that in region i. It is useful to note that back migration (i.e., $M_t^i < 0$) from region j to region i occurs if and only if

$$M_t^i < 0 \Leftrightarrow \frac{N_t^i}{N_t^j} < \frac{\Theta^i Z^i}{\Theta^j Z^j} \Leftrightarrow \frac{\Theta^j Z^j}{N_t^j} < \frac{\Theta^i Z^i}{N_t^i}. \qquad (3.15)$$

Therefore, there is a unique value of the relative population size N_t^i/N_t^j at which there is no migration (i.e., $M_t^i = 0$), and this value

---

[5]One can allow for a migration cost $\chi > 0$, in which case migration from region i to region j at time t implies $u_t^i = u_t^j - \chi$.

is given by[6]

$$M_t^i = 0 \Leftrightarrow \frac{N_t^i}{N_t^j} = \frac{\Theta^i Z^i}{\Theta^j Z^j} \Leftrightarrow \frac{\Theta^j Z^j}{N_t^j} = \frac{\Theta^i Z^i}{N_t^i}. \tag{3.16}$$

In summary, the pattern of migration is determined by the relative population size N_t^i/N_t^j, the relative land supply Z^i/Z^j, and the relative hunting-gathering productivity θ^i/θ^j between the two regions.

3.2   Population Dynamics of the Malthusian Economy

Substituting (3.7) into (3.6) yields the population growth rate in region i at time t as

$$\frac{\Delta N_t^i}{N_t^i} = \frac{\gamma}{\rho}\theta^i l^\alpha \left(\frac{Z^i}{N_t^i}\right)^{1-\alpha} \left(1 - \frac{M_t^i}{N_t^i}\right)^\alpha - 1, \tag{3.17}$$

which is decreasing in the level of migration M_t^i for a given N_t^i. Then, we substitute (3.13) into (3.17) to derive

$$\frac{\Delta N_t^i}{N_t^i} = \frac{\gamma}{\rho}\Theta^i Z^i \left(\frac{l}{\Theta^i Z^i + \Theta^j Z^j}\right)^\alpha \frac{(N_t^i + N_t^j)^\alpha}{N_t^i} - 1. \tag{3.18}$$

Similarly, the population growth rate in region j can be derived as

$$\frac{\Delta N_t^j}{N_t^j} = \frac{\gamma}{\rho}\theta^j l^\alpha \left(\frac{Z^j}{N_t^j}\right)^{1-\alpha} \left(1 + \frac{M_t^i}{N_t^j}\right)^\alpha - 1$$

$$= \frac{\gamma}{\rho}\Theta^j Z^j \left(\frac{l}{\Theta^i Z^i + \Theta^j Z^j}\right)^\alpha \frac{(N_t^i + N_t^j)^\alpha}{N_t^j} - 1. \tag{3.19}$$

Setting $\Delta N_t^i = 0$ in (3.18) yields

$$N^j = \left[\frac{N^i}{\frac{\gamma}{\rho}\Theta^i Z^i \left(\frac{l}{\Theta^i Z^i + \Theta^j Z^j}\right)^\alpha}\right]^{1/\alpha} - N^i. \tag{3.20}$$

---

[6]In the case of a positive migration cost, this unique value becomes a range of parameter values.

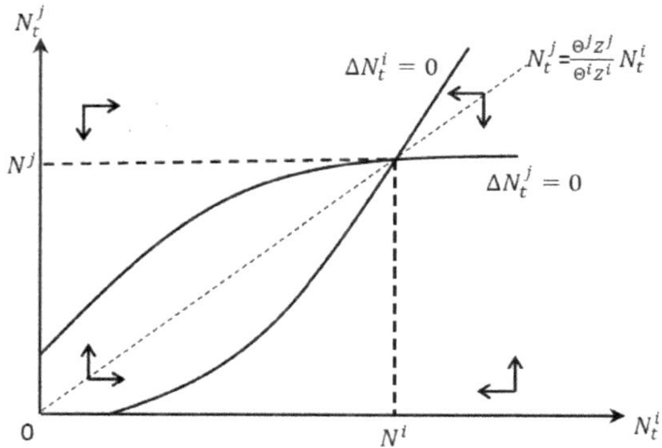

Figure 3.1. Phase diagram.

Similarly, setting $\Delta N_t^j = 0$ in (3.19) yields

$$N^i = \left[\frac{N^j}{\frac{\gamma}{\rho}\Theta^j Z^j \left(\frac{l}{\Theta^i Z^i + \Theta^j Z^j}\right)^\alpha}\right]^{1/\alpha} - N^j. \qquad (3.21)$$

Figure 3.1 plots the phase diagram and shows that the economy always converges to a stable steady state.[7]

From (3.18) and (3.19), the steady-state relative population level between the regions is

$$\frac{N^i}{N^j} = \frac{\Theta^i Z^i}{\Theta^j Z^j}. \qquad (3.22)$$

Then, the steady-state population level in region i is

$$N^i = \left(\frac{\gamma l^\alpha}{\rho}\right)^{1/(1-\alpha)} \Theta^i Z^i, \qquad (3.23)$$

which is increasing in fertility preference γ, labor supply l, region i's productivity θ^i, and land supply Z^i but decreasing in fertility cost ρ.

---

[7]It can be shown that N_t^i and N_t^j first adjust to the steady-state ratio N^i/N^j in (3.22), at which point $M_t^i = 0$ as shown in (3.16), and then gradually move along $N_t^j = \frac{\Theta^j Z^j}{\Theta^i Z^i} N_t^i$ toward the steady-state values N^i in (3.23) and N^j in (3.24).

Similarly, the steady-state population level in region j is

$$N^j = \left(\frac{\gamma l^\alpha}{\rho}\right)^{1/(1-\alpha)} \Theta^j Z^j, \tag{3.24}$$

which is also increasing in fertility preference γ, labor supply l, region j's productivity θ^j, and land supply Z^j but decreasing in fertility cost ρ.

The reason why the steady-state population level in a region does not depend on the productivity and supply of natural resources in the other region is that there is no migration in the long run. To see this, we substitute (3.23) and (3.24) into (3.13) to derive the steady-state level of migration:

$$M^i = 0. \tag{3.25}$$

In other words, the level of migration M_t^i becomes zero as the relative population size N_t^i/N_t^j adjusts to the unique value $\Theta^i Z^i/(\Theta^j Z^j)$ in (3.16).

In summary, the human population in each region i converges to a stable steady-state population size, which is increasing in fertility preference γ, labor supply l, hunting-gathering productivity θ^i, and supply Z^i of natural resources in the region but decreasing in fertility cost ρ. Furthermore, the steady-state level of migration is zero. Given that we have understood the population dynamics of our Malthusian growth model, we now explore the first out-of-Africa migration of our ancestors.

3.2.1 The first migration out of Africa

Before the first hominin migrated out of Africa, the other continents were initially uninhabited. If archaic humans were to remain in Africa and never migrated, then the other continents would remain uninhabited. In this case, the growth rate of human population would be

$$\frac{\Delta N_t^a}{N_t^a} = \frac{\gamma}{\rho}\theta^a l^\alpha \left(\frac{Z^a}{N_t^a}\right)^{1-\alpha} - 1, \tag{3.26}$$

where region a represents Africa. Given initial population N_0^a in Africa, the population size N_t^a converges to

$$N^a = \left(\frac{\gamma l^\alpha}{\rho}\right)^{1/(1-\alpha)} \Theta^a Z^a, \tag{3.27}$$

which depends on the productivity $\Theta^a \equiv (\theta^a)^{1/(1-\alpha)}$ and supply Z^a of natural resources in Africa alone.

However, migration should occur because the following condition from (3.14) holds:

$$\frac{\Theta^e Z^e}{N_t^e} > \frac{\Theta^a Z^a}{N_t^a}, \tag{3.28}$$

where region e represents Eurasia. In the presence of migration from Africa to Eurasia, the population growth rate in Africa would be

$$\frac{\Delta N_t^a}{N_t^a} = \frac{\gamma}{\rho}\theta^a l^\alpha \left(\frac{Z^a}{N_t^a}\right)^{1-\alpha} \left(1 - \frac{M_t^a}{N_t^a}\right)^\alpha - 1, \tag{3.29}$$

which is initially lower than the case without migration in (3.26). However, the population growth rate in Eurasia is now positive due to migration and given by

$$\frac{\Delta N_t^e}{N_t^e} = \frac{\gamma}{\rho}\theta^e l^\alpha \left(\frac{Z^e}{N_t^e}\right)^{1-\alpha} \left(1 + \frac{M_t^a}{N_t^e}\right)^\alpha - 1. \tag{3.30}$$

As shown in the previous section, the total population in the two continents converges to

$$N^a + N^e = \left(\frac{\gamma l^\alpha}{\rho}\right)^{1/(1-\alpha)} [\Theta^a Z^a + \Theta^e Z^e], \tag{3.31}$$

which is greater than the case without migration in (3.27). Therefore, migration gives rise to a larger human population in the long run.

3.3   Summary and Discussion

In this chapter, we have explored prehistoric human migration in a multi-region Malthusian growth model. Our findings can be summarized as follows. Prehistoric migration patterns depend on the relative population size, the relative land supply, and the relative hunting-gathering productivity between regions. Furthermore, prehistoric migrations of archaic humans gave rise to a larger human population, which has important implications for human evolution, as we show in subsequent chapters. In the following chapter, we explore the extinction of archaic humans and the survival of early modern humans.

Chapter 4

Extinction of Archaic Humans

In the previous chapter, we explore the migration of early humans. When early modern humans migrated, they encountered other human species. This chapter explores how archaic humans became extinct. For most of the past 300,000 years, early modern humans and archaic humans, such as Neanderthals and Denisovans, coexisted.[1] These archaic humans only became extinct after early modern humans migrated from Africa to Asia and Europe around 70,000–50,000 years ago.[2] Neanderthals lived in Eurasia and became extinct

---

[1]There is clear evidence for interbreeding between early modern humans and these archaic humans, whose DNA is still present in modern humans; see, e.g., Prufer *et al.* (2014, 2017). Due to this interbreeding, some studies suggest that Neanderthals and Denisovans should be considered subspecies of *Homo sapiens*. It is not clear which species was their last common ancestor. Some studies suggest *Homo heidelbergensis* as the last common ancestor of early modern humans and Neanderthals, whereas a recent study by Feng *et al.* (2024) suggests that the roughly 1 million-year-old Yunxian Man in Hubei, China, "represents a population lying close to the last common ancestor of [early modern humans and Denisovans]."

[2]See Reich (2018). There is also evidence for earlier waves of early modern humans' migration out of Africa starting from as early as over 200,000 years ago, but these early modern humans did not seem to have survived and seemed to have been outcompeted by other archaic humans; see Harvati *et al.* (2019). There is also evidence that early modern humans were already present in China around 120,000–80,000 years ago; see Liu *et al.* (2015).

about 40,000 years ago,[3] whereas Denisovans lived in Asia and possibly became extinct as late as 32,000 years ago.[4]

In this chapter, we extend the baseline Malthusian growth model in Chapter 1 to incorporate natural selection of different human species.[5] Then, we apply the growth-theoretic framework to explore the conditions under which the population dynamics of one human species may cause the extinction of another human species. Specifically, we consider two groups of humans, who engage in hunting-gathering and compete for land. The division of land between the two groups is determined by a conflict success function, which depends on the relative population size. In this case, the larger group of humans can occupy a larger area of land for hunting-gathering. Therefore, the expansion of one population causes the other population to shrink or even become extinct, depending on the intensity of competition between the two groups (which is captured by a parameter in the conflict success function that is the elasticity of the relative share of land with respect to the relative population size). If this elasticity is less than unity, then the two populations coexist in the long run. However, if this elasticity is equal to unity, then the population that has a weaker fertility preference, a higher fertility cost, a lower level of hunting-gathering productivity, and a lower supply of labor eventually becomes extinct.

The above result has the following implications for the Neanderthal extinction. Given the lack of prehistoric data, we do not know whether early modern humans or Neanderthals were more productive hunter-gatherers. On the one hand, early modern humans seemed to have a cognitive advantage (due to possibly a different brain

---

[3]See Higham *et al.* (2014).

[4]See Xia *et al.* (2024).

[5]This chapter is based on Chu (2023). Section 3.4 in Chu (2023) provides a discussion of existing hypotheses on the Neanderthal extinction. See also Horan *et al.* (2005) and Keskin *et al.* (2022) for other economic studies of the Neanderthal extinction.

organization despite their smaller brain size) over Neanderthals.[6] On the other hand, Neanderthals had more robust bodies than early modern humans.[7] What we know from existing archeological evidence is that early modern humans had a higher fertility rate than Neanderthals.[8] The analysis in this chapter shows that even if Neanderthals were more productive hunter-gatherers than early modern humans, the lower fertility of the Neanderthals could be caused by a higher fertility cost[9] and/or a weaker fertility preference[10] and give rise to their extinction when competing with early modern humans.[11] In this scenario, our model predicts that early modern humans enjoyed a higher fertility rate by enduring lower consumption than Neanderthals. This theoretical prediction is consistent with the empirical observation that Neanderthals had more robust skeletons/muscular bodies and a larger brain size than early modern humans.

4.1 A Malthusian Growth Model with Natural Selection of Human Species

Consider two species of humans indexed by superscript $i \in \{a, s\}$. The human species s denotes *Homo sapiens*, whereas the human species a refers to an archaic human species, such as the Neanderthals. Both groups of humans are hunter-gatherers. There is a

---

[6]See Reardon (2022).

[7]See Horan *et al.* (2005).

[8]See Trinkaus (2011).

[9]According to Trinkaus (1986), Neanderthals had a longer gestation length of at least 11 months.

[10]A weaker fertility preference implies a smaller weight in the utility function on fertility relative to consumption. Lagerlof (2007) argues that given their more muscular bodies and larger brain size than early modern humans, Neanderthals required higher food consumption.

[11]According to Banks *et al.* (2008), the Neanderthal extinction followed a reduction in their geographic range due to competition with early modern humans and their geographic expansion.

fixed amount of land Z, and the larger group of humans occupies a larger share of land.

4.1.1 Endogenous fertility

In each human group $i \in \{a, s\}$, there are N_t^i agents at time t. As before, each agent lives for two periods, and each adult agent of group i at time t has the following utility function:

$$u_t^i = (1 - \gamma^i) \ln c_t^i + \gamma^i \ln n_t^i, \tag{4.1}$$

where $\gamma^i \in (0, 1)$ measures human species i's preference for fertility and n_t^i is the number of children per adult agent in this group. Raising children is costly, and the level of consumption c_t^i net of the fertility cost is given by

$$c_t^i = y_t^i - \rho^i n_t^i, \tag{4.2}$$

where $\rho^i > 0$ determines human species i's fertility cost and y_t^i is the per capita level of food production in this group.

Substituting (4.2) into (4.1), we derive the fertility rate n_t^i of group i as

$$n_t^i = \frac{\gamma^i}{\rho^i} y_t^i \tag{4.3}$$

and consumption as $c_t^i = (1 - \gamma^i) y_t^i$. Each adult agent in group i has n_t^i children, and the number of adult agents at time t is N_t^i. Therefore, the law of motion for the adult population size of group i is

$$N_{t+1}^i = n_t^i N_t^i = \frac{\gamma^i}{\rho^i} y_t^i N_t^i, \tag{4.4}$$

and its growth rate at time t is

$$\frac{\Delta N_t^i}{N_t^i} = \frac{\gamma^i}{\rho^i} y_t^i - 1, \tag{4.5}$$

which will be referred to as the population growth rate of group i.

4.1.2 Hunting-gathering

Total food production from hunting-gathering in group $i \in \{a, s\}$ is given by

$$Y_t^i = \theta^i (l^i N_t^i)^\alpha (Z_t^i)^{1-\alpha}, \tag{4.6}$$

where $l^i N_t^i$ and Z_t^i are, respectively, the total amount of labor and land devoted to hunting-gathering by group i. Individual labor supply $l^i > 0$ is exogenous and could differ across human species. The parameters $\theta^i > 0$ and $\alpha \in (0, 1)$ measure, respectively, hunting-gathering productivity of group i and labor intensity of the hunting-gathering process. Each agent in group i receives y_t^i units of food production, given by

$$y_t^i = \theta^i (l^i)^\alpha \left(\frac{Z_t^i}{N_t^i} \right)^{1-\alpha}. \tag{4.7}$$

4.1.3 Land division

We follow the literature on the macrotechnology of conflict to assume the presence of a conflict success function[12] for resource competition and the division of land between the two groups of humans. Specifically, the amount of land occupied by group i is specified as follows:

$$Z_t^i = \frac{(N_t^i)^\phi}{(N_t^i)^\phi + (N_t^j)^\phi} Z, \tag{4.8}$$

where the parameter $Z > 0$ denotes the total amount of land and the parameter $\phi \in [0, 1]$ is known as the decisiveness parameter.[13] If $\phi = 0$, then the amount of land is equally divided between the two groups, such that $Z_t^i = Z/2$. As ϕ increases, the ratio of land

---

[12]See Hirshleifer (1991, 2000).
[13]Population dynamics would become unstable if $\phi > 1$.

becomes more sensitive to the population ratio:

$$\frac{Z_t^i}{Z_t^j} = \left(\frac{N_t^i}{N_t^j}\right)^\phi, \tag{4.9}$$

which shows that ϕ parameterizes the elasticity of the land ratio with respect to the population ratio. As we will show, this elasticity determines whether the Neanderthal extinction occurs or not.

4.2   Population Dynamics

Given an initial level of population N_0^i, the population growth rate of group i is

$$\frac{\Delta N_t^i}{N_t^i} = \frac{\gamma^i}{\rho^i}\theta^i(l^i)^\alpha \left[\frac{(N_t^i)^\phi}{(N_t^i)^\phi + (N_t^j)^\phi}\frac{Z}{N_t^i}\right]^{1-\alpha} - 1, \tag{4.10}$$

which uses (4.5), (4.7), and (4.8). There are three scenarios: $\phi = 0$, $\phi \in (0,1)$, and $\phi = 1$.

4.2.1   Population dynamics without resource competition

First, we consider $\phi = 0$. In this case, the dynamics of the two populations becomes independent, and (4.10) simplifies to

$$\frac{\Delta N_t^i}{N_t^i} = \frac{\gamma^i}{\rho^i}\theta^i(l^i)^\alpha \left(\frac{Z}{2N_t^i}\right)^{1-\alpha} - 1. \tag{4.11}$$

Figure 4.1 shows that, as in Chapter 1, given any initial level N_0^i, the population size N_t^i converges to a unique and stable steady state:

$$N^i = \left[\frac{\gamma^i}{\rho^i}\theta^i(l^i)^\alpha\right]^{1/(1-\alpha)}\frac{Z}{2}, \tag{4.12}$$

which shows that the steady-state level of population i is decreasing in its fertility cost ρ^i but increasing in its fertility preference γ^i,

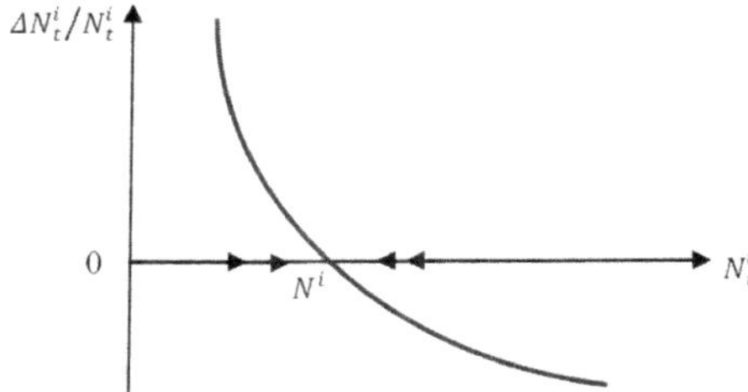

Figure 4.1. Phase diagram for $\phi = 0$.

hunting productivity θ^i, labor supply l^i, and the total amount of land Z. Here, the positive effects of hunting productivity θ^i, labor supply l^i, and land Z on fertility capture the Malthusian mechanism as before. Imposing $\Delta N_t^i = 0$ on (4.5) yields the steady-state level of food output per capita, given by $y^i = \rho^i/\gamma^i$, and the steady-state level of consumption per capita, given by $c^i = (1 - \gamma^i)y^i = \rho^i(1 - \gamma^i)/\gamma^i$. The steady-state levels of food output and consumption per capita are increasing in fertility cost ρ^i and decreasing in fertility preference γ^i as before.

4.2.2 Population dynamics with resource competition

Second, we consider $\phi \in (0, 1)$. In this case, the dynamics of the two populations depend on each other. Setting $\Delta N_t^i = 0$ in (4.10) yields

$$N^i = \left[\frac{\gamma^i}{\rho^i} \theta^i (l^i)^\alpha \right]^{1/(1-\alpha)} \frac{(N^i)^\phi}{(N^i)^\phi + (N^j)^\phi} Z, \qquad (4.13)$$

which can be re-expressed as

$$N^j = \left\{ \left[\frac{\gamma^i}{\rho^i} \theta^i (l^i)^\alpha \right]^{1/(1-\alpha)} \frac{Z}{(N^i)^{1-\phi}} - (N^i)^\phi \right\}^{1/\phi}. \qquad (4.14)$$

Similarly, setting $\Delta N_t^j = 0$ yields

$$N^i = \left\{ \left[\frac{\gamma^j}{\rho^j} \theta^j (l^j)^\alpha \right]^{1/(1-\alpha)} \frac{Z}{(N^j)^{1-\phi}} - (N^j)^\phi \right\}^{1/\phi}. \qquad (4.15)$$

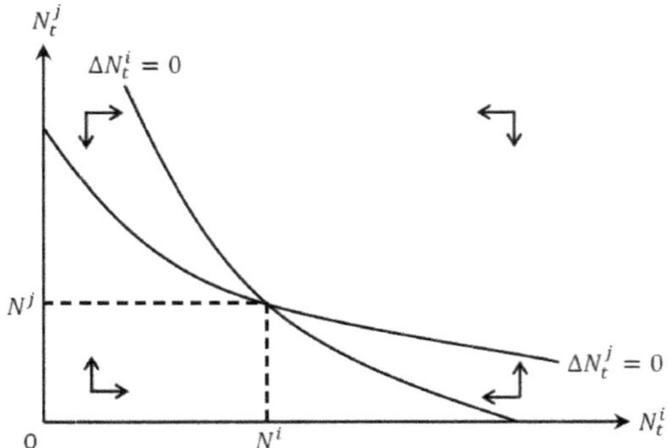

Figure 4.2. Phase diagram for $\phi \in (0,1)$.

Figure 4.2 plots (4.14) and (4.15) along with the dynamics of N_t^i and N_t^j in a phase diagram.

Figure 4.2 shows that given any initial levels of population N_0^i and N_0^j, the population size N_t^i converges to a unique and stable steady-state value, given by

$$N^i = \left[\frac{\gamma^i}{\rho^i}\theta^i(l^i)^\alpha\right]^{1/(1-\alpha)} \left[1 + \left(\frac{N^j}{N^i}\right)^\phi\right]^{-1} Z, \qquad (4.16)$$

where the population ratio is given by

$$\frac{N^i}{N^j} = \left[\frac{\gamma^i\theta^i}{\gamma^j\theta^j}\left(\frac{l^i}{l^j}\right)^\alpha \frac{\rho^j}{\rho^i}\right]^{1/[(1-\alpha)(1-\phi)]}. \qquad (4.17)$$

Substituting (4.17) into (4.16) yields

$$N^i = \frac{\left[\frac{\gamma^i}{\rho^i}\theta^i(l^i)^\alpha\right]^{1/(1-\alpha)}}{1 + \left[\frac{\gamma^j\theta^j}{\gamma^i\theta^i}\left(\frac{l^j}{l^i}\right)^\alpha \frac{\rho^i}{\rho^j}\right]^{\phi/[(1-\alpha)(1-\phi)]}} Z.$$

As before, the steady-state level of population i is decreasing in its own fertility cost ρ^i and increasing in its own fertility preference γ^i, hunting-gathering productivity θ^i, labor supply l^i, and the total amount of land Z. Interestingly, the steady-state level of population i is now increasing in the other population's fertility cost

ρ^j and decreasing in their fertility preference γ^j, hunting-gathering productivity θ^j, and labor supply l^j. Intuitively, as the other population j becomes larger, the amount of land captured by population i becomes smaller, which in turn reduces its population size in the Malthusian economy. However, both populations continue to coexist in the long run. Finally, we impose $\Delta N_t^i = 0$ on (4.5) to derive the steady-state level of food output per capita as $y^i = \rho^i/\gamma^i$ and the steady-state level of consumption per capita as $c^i = \rho^i(1 - \gamma^i)/\gamma^i$, which are both increasing in own fertility cost ρ^i and decreasing in own fertility preference γ^i for the same reason as before.

4.2.3 Population dynamics with population extinction

Third, we consider $\phi = 1$. In this case, (4.10) simplifies to

$$\frac{\Delta N_t^i}{N_t^i} = \frac{\gamma^i}{\rho^i}\theta^i(l^i)^\alpha \left(\frac{Z}{N_t^i + N_t^j}\right)^{1-\alpha} - 1, \tag{4.18}$$

which shows that

$$\frac{\Delta N_t^i}{N_t^i} > \frac{\Delta N_t^j}{N_t^j} \Leftrightarrow \frac{\gamma^i}{\rho^i}\theta^i(l^i)^\alpha > \frac{\gamma^j}{\rho^j}\theta^j(l^j)^\alpha. \tag{4.19}$$

Without loss of generality, let's assume that $\gamma^i\theta^i(l^i)^\alpha/\rho^i > \gamma^j\theta^j(l^j)^\alpha/\rho^j$. Setting $\Delta N_t^i = 0$ in (4.18) yields

$$N^j = \left[\frac{\gamma^i}{\rho^i}\theta^i(l^i)^\alpha\right]^{1/(1-\alpha)} Z - N^i. \tag{4.20}$$

Similarly, setting $\Delta N_t^j = 0$ yields

$$N^i = \left[\frac{\gamma^j}{\rho^j}\theta^j(l^j)^\alpha\right]^{1/(1-\alpha)} Z - N^j. \tag{4.21}$$

Figure 4.3 plots (4.20) and (4.21) along with the dynamics of N_t^i and N_t^j in a phase diagram.

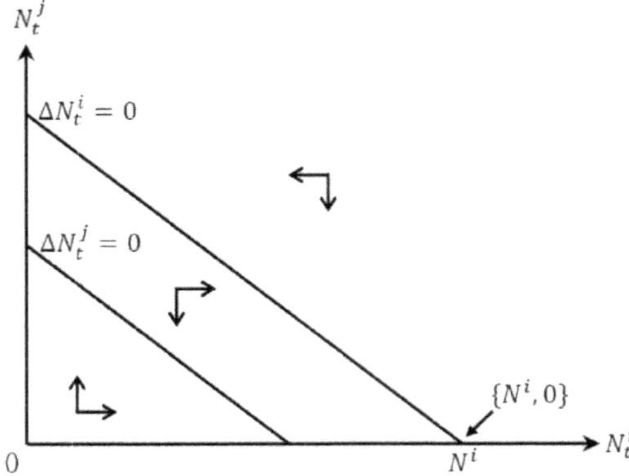

Figure 4.3. Phase diagram for $\phi = 1$.

Figure 4.3 shows that given any initial levels of population N_0^i and N_0^j, the population sizes $\{N_t^i, N_t^j\}$ converge to $\{N^i, 0\}$. Suppose $\Delta N_0^i / N_0^i > \Delta N_0^j / N_0^j > 0$ at the initial population levels $\{N_0^i, N_0^j\}$. Then, the two populations are both initially growing. As both N_t^i and N_t^j increase, their growth rates decrease over time. Eventually, $\Delta N_t^j / N_t^j$ becomes negative while $\Delta N_t^i / N_t^i$ remains positive. At this stage, the size N_t^i of population i keeps rising, whereas the size N_t^j of population j shrinks over time. In the long run, the size N_t^j of population j shrinks toward zero, and the size N_t^i of population i converges to the following steady state:

$$N^i = \left[\frac{\gamma^i}{\rho^i}\theta^i (l^i)^\alpha\right]^{1/(1-\alpha)} Z, \tag{4.22}$$

which, as before, is decreasing in fertility cost ρ^i but increasing in fertility preference γ^i, hunting-gathering productivity θ^i, labor supply l^i, and the amount of land Z.

The transition path of consumption per capita is given by

$$c_t^i = (1 - \gamma^i)y_t^i = (1 - \gamma^i)\theta^i (l^i)^\alpha \left(\frac{Z}{N_t^i + N_t^j}\right)^{1-\alpha}, \tag{4.23}$$

which is increasing in hunting-gathering productivity θ^i and labor supply l^i but decreasing in fertility preference γ^i. Given the survival of *Homo sapiens* and the extinction of archaic humans, our model requires $\gamma^s \theta^s (l^s)^\alpha / \rho^s > \gamma^a \theta^a (l^a)^\alpha / \rho^a$. Evidence suggests that Neanderthals had more robust skeletons and muscular bodies, which may imply $\theta^a (l^a)^\alpha > \theta^s (l^s)^\alpha$. These two conditions together imply that γ^s / ρ^s must be significantly larger than γ^a / ρ^a in order for early modern humans to have a higher fertility rate than Neanderthals. In other words, the lower fertility of the Neanderthals could be caused by their higher fertility cost ρ^a and/or their weaker fertility preference γ^a despite their potentially higher hunting-gathering productivity $\theta^a (l^a)^\alpha$. However, early modern humans could afford higher fertility only by enduring lower consumption. Therefore, Neanderthals should have enjoyed a higher level of consumption than early modern humans before their extinction (i.e., $c_t^a > c_t^s$, for all t, before $N_t^a \to 0$), which is consistent with the fact that Neanderthals had more robust skeletons and muscular bodies than early modern humans.

Using a matrix population model, Degioanni *et al.* (2019) provide evidence that the lower fertility rate of Neanderthals caused their extinction. However, why did the Neanderthals have a lower fertility rate? In our Malthusian growth model, fertility decisions are made by optimizing agents of each human species. This microfoundation for the fertility rate enables us to explore how the fertility preference and the cost of fertility could dominate hunting-gathering productivity and labor supply in determining the endogenous fertility rates of different human species and how the intensity of resource competition determines whether the Neanderthal extinction occurs or not.

4.2.4 Hybridization in human evolution

Modern humans carry some proportion of Neanderthal-derived DNA.[14] For example, Prufer *et al.* (2014) report estimates that range from 1.5% to 2.1%, whereas a subsequent study by Prufer *et al.*

---

[14]Modern humans also carry some proportion of Denisovan-derived DNA; see, e.g., Krause *et al.* (2010).

(2017) reports more precise estimates of 2.3–2.6% for East Asians and 1.8–2.4% for Western Eurasians. Therefore, there is also a hypothesis of Neanderthal extinction caused by interbreeding with early modern humans, which however seemed to be a minor contributor to the Neanderthal extinction according to Timmermann (2020).

Chu (2024b) introduces interbreeding between early modern humans and the Neanderthals to the Malthusian model in the previous section. In this case, a share $\sigma^i \in (0,1)$ of the N_t^i adult agents leaves group i at every time t and engages in interbreeding with the other human group j. In this case, the population growth rate of group $i \in \{a, s\}$ in (4.18) becomes

$$\frac{\Delta N_t^i}{N_t^i} = (1 - \sigma^i)\frac{\gamma^i}{\rho^i}\theta^i(l^i)^\alpha \left(\frac{Z}{N_t}\right)^{1-\alpha} - 1, \qquad (4.24)$$

where N_t is the total population size at time t. Given that $\sigma^a N_t^a + \sigma^s N_t^s$ agents from the two groups interbreed at every time t and join the new hybrid group h, the population growth rate of this hybrid human group is

$$\frac{\Delta N_t^h}{N_t^h} = \frac{\gamma^h}{\rho^h}\theta^h(l^h)^\alpha \left(\frac{Z}{N_t}\right)^{1-\alpha} \left(1 + \frac{\sigma^a N_t^a + \sigma^s N_t^s}{N_t^h}\right) - 1, \qquad (4.25)$$

where $N_t = N_t^h + N_t^a + N_t^s$. Chu (2024b) derives the population dynamics of this extended model and shows that the archaic human group a becomes extinct as before, whereas the group s of early modern humans survives, given $(1 - \sigma^s)\gamma^s\theta^s(l^s)^\alpha/\rho^s > (1 - \sigma^a)\gamma^a\theta^a(l^a)^\alpha/\rho^a$. Furthermore, despite the parameter assumption $(1 - \sigma^s)\gamma^s\theta^s(l^s)^\alpha/\rho^s > \gamma^h\theta^h(l^h)^\alpha/\rho^h$, the hybrid human group h also survives in the human population in the long run due to the continued hybridization with early modern humans.

The above finding may help explain the fact that modern humans still carry some Neanderthal-derived DNA. In other words, those modern humans with Neanderthal DNA correspond to descendants of the hybrid population in our model, whereas those modern humans without Neanderthal DNA correspond to non-hybrid descendants of the initial *Homo sapiens* population. It was previously believed that only non-Africans carry Neanderthal DNA; however, there is recent evidence that all modern humans, including Africans, carry Neanderthal DNA.[15] Chu (2024b) shows that if $\gamma^h \theta^h (l^h)^\alpha / \rho^h > (1 - \sigma^s) \gamma^s \theta^s (l^s)^\alpha / \rho^s$, then the hybrid population dominates the human population in the long run as the only surviving human species, which captures the possible case that all modern humans are hybrid descendants of archaic and early modern humans.

4.3 Summary and Discussion

In this chapter, we have extended the canonical Malthusian growth model to explore natural selection of human species. Given the scarcity of natural resources and the ability of a larger group of humans to capture more natural resources, the expansion of one population causes the other population to shrink in a Malthusian economy. However, the less fertile species does not necessarily become extinct. Whether the extinction of a human species occurs or not depends on the elasticity of the relative share of land with respect to the relative population size, which captures the intensity of resource competition between human species. If this elasticity is below unity, then the two populations coexist even in the long run. However, if the elasticity is equal to unity, then the less fertile species eventually becomes extinct due to a high intensity of resource competition, which could be triggered by climate change or natural catastrophe (e.g., volcanic eruptions). Chu (2023) extended this analysis to an arbitrary number of human species and showed that only one human species survives in the long run (as in the case of *Homo sapiens*) under a unitary elasticity of the relative share of land with respect to the relative population size. The following chapter explores how the surviving early modern humans eventually evolved from hunting-gathering tribes to agricultural settlements.

---

[15]There is evidence that Africans may also carry Neanderthal DNA of up to 0.3%; see Price (2020).

Part II
Agricultural Era

Chapter 5

The Neolithic Revolution

In Chapter 4, we explore how *Homo sapiens* became the only surviving human species. For most of their history, early modern humans were hunter-gatherers. The Neolithic Revolution (the transition from hunting-gathering to agriculture) occurred in the Fertile Crescent, with the cultivation of wheat and barley and the domestication of sheep and goats about 12,000 years ago, and then independently in other parts of the world.[1] For example, rice cultivation and domestication occurred in ancient China as early as 9,400 years ago in the Yangtze River Valley,[2] and this agricultural transition planted the seed of the birth of the Chinese civilization.[3] "The Neolithic Revolution had an enduring effect on humanity. In a matter of only a few thousand years, the majority of humans abandoned their nomadic lifestyle."[4] Was this agricultural transition of human society inevitable? If not, what are the different conditions that could have potentially made the agricultural transition more or less likely to occur?

---

[1]See Barker (2006) for a discussion of archeological evidence for the origins of agriculture.

[2]See Zuo *et al.* (2017).

[3]In Chinese mythology, Shennong is credited as the clan to have first adopted agriculture and invented various agricultural tools in ancient China.

[4]Galor (2022, p. 120).

43

In this chapter, we extend the Malthusian growth model to capture the economic evolution of human society from hunting-gathering to agriculture.[5] The extended Malthusian growth model features two stages of food production. The first stage is hunting-gathering as before, whereas the second stage is agricultural production. Human society evolves across these two stages as the size of the population grows. Given the Malthusian environment, the population may stop growing at any stage and never reach the next threshold under endogenous population growth that is determined by the fertility decisions of optimizing agents in our microfounded model. If the population size fails to reach the agricultural threshold, then the population remains in a hunting-gathering Malthusian trap. If the population size reaches this threshold, then an agricultural society emerges; therefore, both the Boserupian and Malthusian forces are present in our extended Malthusian growth model.[6]

Our growth-theoretic analysis shows that the Neolithic Revolution occurs under the following conditions: a high level of agricultural productivity, a low cost of fertility, and a strong preference for fertility. Some studies, such as those by Olsson and Hibbs (2005), Ashraf and Galor (2011), Ang (2015), and Chu and Xu (2024), provide empirical evidence that high agricultural productivity indeed leads to an earlier transition to agriculture. After an agricultural society emerges, the economy eventually becomes completely agricultural and converges to an agricultural Malthusian trap in the long run.

5.1 A Static Model of Economic Evolution

The model of agricultural transition is based on Locay (1989); see also Baker (2008), who finds empirical support for this model using

---

[5]This chapter is based on Chu and Xu (2024). See Weisdorf (2005) for an early survey of this literature and Baker (2008), Dow *et al.* (2009), Weisdorf (2011), Dow and Reed (2015, 2022), and Choi (2019) for more recent studies.

[6]Boserup (1965) argues that agricultural methods depend on the population size. Her idea has been extended to the case in which the transition to agriculture also depends on the population size; see Cohen (1977).

historical data on the incidence of agriculture. We first present a static version of the model with an exogenous level of population before extending the model to a dynamic version with endogenous population growth. In the first stage, the population engages in hunting-gathering. In the second stage, an agricultural society emerges. The population consists of N identical agents.[7] Each agent is endowed with l units of labor, which can be allocated to hunting-gathering l_H or farming l_F. Therefore, the labor constraint faced by each agent is

$$l_H + l_F = l. \tag{5.1}$$

There is also a fixed amount of land denoted as Z, which can be used for hunting-gathering or farming.

5.1.1 Hunting-gathering production

Hunting-gathering takes place in available land that is not occupied for farming. We use $\bar{l}_H$ to denote the average amount of labor endowment devoted to hunting-gathering. Then, total food production from hunting-gathering is given by

$$H = \theta(\bar{l}_H N)^\alpha (Z_H)^{1-\alpha}, \tag{5.2}$$

where $\bar{l}_H N$ and $Z_H \leq Z$ are, respectively, the total amount of labor and land devoted to hunting-gathering. As before, the parameters $\theta > 0$ and $\alpha \in (0, 1)$ measure, respectively, the productivity and labor intensity of the hunting-gathering process. An agent, who contributes l_H units of labor to hunting-gathering, receives a proportional share of food production given by

$$h = \frac{l_H}{\bar{l}_H N} \theta(\bar{l}_H N)^\alpha (Z_H)^{1-\alpha}, \tag{5.3}$$

in which the agent takes $\bar{l}_H$ and Z_H as given.

---

[7]In this chapter, we use N to denote the exogenous level of population in the static model and N^* to denote the steady-state level of population in the dynamic model.

5.1.2 Agricultural production

Farming also requires both labor and land. The farming production of an agent, who devotes l_F units of labor to farming, is

$$f = \varphi(l_F)^\beta z^{1-\beta}, \tag{5.4}$$

where the parameters $\varphi > 0$ and $\beta \in (0,1)$ measure, respectively, the productivity and labor intensity in agriculture. z is the amount of land used by the agent. We follow Baker (2008) to assume a fixed ratio ϱ of land to farming labor given by

$$z = \varrho l_F, \tag{5.5}$$

when agricultural land is not scarce (i.e., $\varrho \bar{l}_F N < Z$); in this case, $f = \varphi \varrho^{1-\beta} l_F$. Weisdorf (2005) argues that this temporary state of constant returns to farming labor, which is also present in the seminal study by North and Thomas (1977), is a reasonable assumption when there is abundant agricultural land. When agricultural land becomes scarce, it is equally divided between agents, i.e.,

$$z = Z/N. \tag{5.6}$$

In this case, there is no more land available for hunting-gathering (i.e., $Z_H = 0$); see North and Thomas (1977) for a discussion on why, with communal property rights on agricultural land, sedentary farmers had better access to land than hunter-gatherers, who mostly had a nomadic lifestyle.

5.1.3 Hunting-gathering versus agriculture

In this section, we explore the evolution of the economy. We begin by imposing the following parameter assumption that ensures agricultural productivity is higher than hunting-gathering productivity: $\varphi > \theta$. The population begins as hunter-gatherers and evolves into an agricultural society. Each agent maximizes consumption c

given by

$$c = y = h + f, \tag{5.7}$$

where y denotes total food production per capita. An agent's decision is to choose labor allocation between hunting-gathering l_H and farming l_F to maximize food production y given by

$$y = h + f = \frac{l_H}{\bar{l}_H N}\theta(\bar{l}_H N)^\alpha(Z_H)^{1-\alpha} + \varphi(l_F)^\beta z^{1-\beta}$$

$$= (l - l_F)\theta\left(\frac{Z_H}{\bar{l}_H N}\right)^{1-\alpha} + \varphi\varrho^{1-\beta}l_F, \tag{5.8}$$

where we have used the resource constraint on labor, $l_H + l_F = l$, and the fixed ratio of land to farming labor, $z = \varrho l_F$. The first-order condition is given by

$$\frac{\partial y}{\partial l_F} = -\theta\left(\frac{Z_H}{\bar{l}_H N}\right)^{1-\alpha} + \varphi\varrho^{1-\beta} = -\theta\left[\frac{Z - \varrho l_F N}{(l - l_F)N}\right]^{1-\alpha} + \varphi\varrho^{1-\beta}, \tag{5.9}$$

where we have invoked symmetry $\{l_H, l_F\} = \{\bar{l}_H, \bar{l}_F\}$ and also used the resource constraint on land $Z_H = Z - \varrho l_F N$. In (5.9), $\varphi\varrho^{1-\beta}$ is the marginal product of farming labor l_F, whereas $\theta\left[\frac{Z-\varrho l_F N}{(l-l_F)N}\right]^{1-\alpha}$ is the average product of hunting-gathering labor $l_H = l - l_F$. In the following sections, we compare these two objects under different population levels.

5.1.4 Stage 1: Hunting-gathering

Equation (5.9) implies that if the following inequality holds:

$$N < \left(\frac{\theta}{\varphi\varrho^{1-\beta}}\right)^{1/(1-\alpha)}\frac{Z}{l}, \tag{5.10}$$

then $\partial y/\partial l_F < 0$ even at $l_F = 0$. In this case, all labor is allocated to hunting-gathering $l_H = l$, and the per capita output of food production is given by

$$y = h = \theta l^{\alpha} \left(\frac{Z}{N}\right)^{1-\alpha}, \tag{5.11}$$

which is increasing in hunting-gathering productivity θ, labor supply l, and the amount of land Z but decreasing in the population size N due to the decreasing returns to labor in hunting-gathering.

5.1.5 Stage 2: From hunting-gathering to agriculture

Equation (5.9) and $\varrho l_F N < Z$ imply that if the following inequalities hold:

$$\left(\frac{\theta}{\varphi \varrho^{1-\beta}}\right)^{1/(1-\alpha)} \frac{Z}{l} < N < \frac{Z}{\varrho l}, \tag{5.12}$$

then $\partial y / \partial l_F = 0$ at some interior values of $\{l_F, l_H\} \in (0, l)$. In this case, the transition from hunting-gathering to agriculture begins. The first inequality shows that a reduction in hunting-gathering productivity θ or an increase in population size N could trigger this transition. In our static model, the reduction in hunting productivity θ captures the extinction of large herding animals, as analyzed by Smith (1975),[8] whereas an exogenous increase in population size N captures the population pressure theory discussed by Cohen (1977). However, as we will show, these results would be quite different in our dynamic model with endogenous population growth.

During the gradual transition from hunting-gathering to agriculture, the per capita output of food production is given by

$$y = h + f = (l - l_F)\theta \left(\frac{Z_H}{\bar{l}_H N}\right)^{1-\alpha} + \varphi \varrho^{1-\beta} l_F = \varphi \varrho^{1-\beta} l, \tag{5.13}$$

which uses $\theta [Z_H/(\bar{l}_H N)]^{1-\alpha} = \varphi \varrho^{1-\beta}$ from (5.9). Equation (5.13) shows that y is increasing in labor supply l and agricultural productivity $\varphi \varrho^{1-\beta}$.

---

[8]Smith (1975) considers a dynamic model of replenishable common resources, in which animal extinction is caused by excessive hunting.

5.1.6 Stage 3: Complete transition to agriculture

When $N > Z/(\varrho l)$, the transition from hunting-gathering to agriculture is complete (i.e., $l_F = l$) because $Z_H = 0$. At this stage, the level of output per capita is given by

$$y = f = \varphi l^\beta \left(\frac{Z}{N}\right)^{1-\beta}, \tag{5.14}$$

which is increasing in agricultural productivity φ, labor supply l, and the amount of land Z but decreasing in the population size N due to the decreasing returns to labor in farming when agricultural land is scarce.

5.1.7 Consumption at different stages

In this section, we summarize the level of consumption per capita at different levels of population as follows:

$$c = y = \begin{cases} h = \theta l^\alpha \left(\frac{Z}{N}\right)^{1-\alpha} & \text{for } N < \left(\frac{\theta}{\varphi \varrho^{1-\beta}}\right)^{1/(1-\alpha)} \frac{Z}{l} \\[2ex] h + f = \varphi \varrho^{1-\beta} l & \text{for } \left(\frac{\theta}{\varphi \varrho^{1-\beta}}\right)^{1/(1-\alpha)} \frac{Z}{l} < N < \frac{Z}{\varrho l} \\[2ex] f = \varphi l^\beta \left(\frac{Z}{N}\right)^{1-\beta} & \text{for } N > \frac{Z}{\varrho l} \end{cases}$$

$$\tag{5.15}$$

Equation (5.15) presents the level of per capita consumption c as population N rises; see Figure 5.1. In summary, c is initially falling due to the decreasing returns to labor in hunting-gathering. Then, consumption c reaches a stationary level (from above) when the gradual transition from hunting-gathering to agriculture begins. Therefore, before the transition to agriculture, hunter-gatherers enjoy a higher level of consumption than the later farmers, which is consistent with archeological evidence; see for example Cohen and Armelagos (1984). However, our model implies that the hunter-gatherers would have experienced a subsequent fall in consumption if they didn't adopt

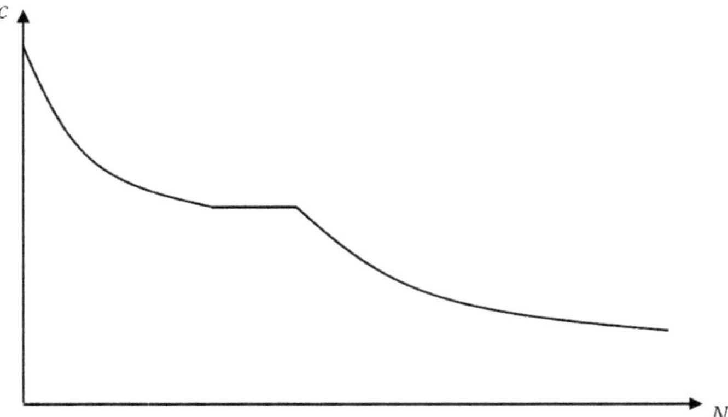

Figure 5.1.   Consumption at different stages.

farming due to the decreasing returns to labor in hunting-gathering.[9]
When the transition from hunting-gathering to agriculture is complete, consumption c begins falling again due to the decreasing
returns to labor in farming when agricultural land is scarce.

5.2   A Dynamic Model with Endogenous Population Growth

Section 5.1 presents a static model with an exogenous level of population. This section extends the model into a dynamic setting with
endogenous population growth. As in previous chapters, each agent
lives for two periods, and each adult agent at time t has the following
utility function:

$$u_t = (1 - \gamma) \ln c_t + \gamma \ln n_t, \tag{5.16}$$

where $\gamma \in (0, 1)$ measures the preference for fertility and n_t is the
agent's number of children. Raising children is costly, and the level

---

[9]See also Galor (2022, pp. 33–34).

of consumption net of the fertility cost is given by

$$c_t = y_t - \rho n_t, \tag{5.17}$$

where $\rho > 0$ determines the cost of fertility. Substituting (5.17) into (5.16), we derive the utility-maximizing level of fertility n_t as

$$n_t = \frac{\gamma}{\rho} y_t, \tag{5.18}$$

and $c_t = (1 - \gamma) y_t$, in which the agent maximizes food output $y_t = h_t + f_t$, as in the previous section.

Each adult agent has n_t children, and the number of adult agents at time t is N_t. Therefore, the law of motion for the adult population size is given by

$$N_{t+1} = n_t N_t = \frac{\gamma}{\rho} y_t N_t, \tag{5.19}$$

and the adult population growth rate at time t is

$$\frac{\Delta N_t}{N_t} = \frac{\gamma}{\rho} y_t - 1 = \frac{\gamma}{\rho} (h_t + f_t) - 1, \tag{5.20}$$

which will be referred to as the population growth rate. In the following, we use the information from the previous section to derive population dynamics.

5.2.1 Stage 1: Hunting-gathering

Given an initial level of population,

$$N_0 < \left(\frac{\theta}{\varphi \varrho^{1-\beta}} \right)^{1/(1-\alpha)} \frac{Z}{l}, \tag{5.21}$$

the human population engages in hunting-gathering only. Substituting (5.11) into (5.20) yields the growth rate of the population as

$$\frac{\Delta N_t}{N_t} = \frac{\gamma}{\rho} \theta l^\alpha \left(\frac{Z}{N_t} \right)^{1-\alpha} - 1, \tag{5.22}$$

which yields the following steady-state population level in a hunting-gathering Malthusian trap:

$$N_H^* = \left(\frac{\gamma}{\rho} \theta l^\alpha \right)^{1/(1-\alpha)} Z. \tag{5.23}$$

5.2.2 Does the Neolithic Revolution occur?

The population remains as hunter-gatherers indefinitely if the following inequality holds:

$$N_H^* < \left(\frac{\theta}{\varphi\varrho^{1-\beta}}\right)^{1/(1-\alpha)} \frac{Z}{l} \Leftrightarrow \frac{\gamma}{\rho}\varphi\varrho^{1-\beta}l < 1. \qquad (5.24)$$

Substituting N_H^* in (5.23) into (5.11) yields $y^* = h^* = \rho/\gamma$, which is increasing in fertility cost ρ and decreasing in the degree γ of fertility preference but independent of hunting productivity θ and land Z. In other words, the population is in a hunting-gathering Malthusian trap, in which higher hunting-gathering productivity θ and more land Z increase the steady-state level of population N_H^* but not the per capita level of hunting-gathering output h^* in the long run.

Alternatively, if $\gamma\varphi\varrho^{1-\beta}l > \rho$, then an agricultural society emerges. Therefore, the transition from hunting-gathering to agriculture occurs under the following conditions: a low fertility cost ρ, a strong fertility preference γ, a high level of agricultural productivity $\varphi\varrho^{1-\beta}$, and a high level of labor supply l. A strong fertility preference γ and a low fertility cost ρ give rise to a higher level of population and make it more likely for the population to cross the threshold for the emergence of agriculture in a Boserupian manner; however, they also reduce the steady-state level of food output per capita $y^* = h^* = \rho/\gamma$ in case the population remains in a hunting-gathering Malthusian trap.

Although a higher level of hunting productivity θ and a larger amount of land Z increase population, they also raise the endogenous threshold for agriculture by making hunting-gathering more attractive. These opposite effects cancel each other, and hence, hunting productivity θ and the amount of land Z do not affect the transition to agriculture. This result stands in stark contrast to the case of exogenous population size.

Finally, high agricultural productivity $\varphi\varrho^{1-\beta}$ reduces the endogenous threshold by making agriculture more attractive, and hence, a high level of agricultural productivity $\varphi\varrho^{1-\beta}$ can trigger the Neolithic

Revolution. This finding is consistent with the empirical evidence given by Olsson and Hibbs (2005), who find that favorable biogeographic conditions can trigger the transition to agriculture. Olsson (2001) examines the archeological evidence in the Jordan Valley and concludes that the abundance of species suitable for agriculture was one of the key reasons for the transition to agriculture. This abundance of agricultural species corresponds to a high level of agricultural productivity in our model.

5.2.3   Stage 2: From hunting-gathering to agriculture

Suppose the population size N_t crosses the first threshold, i.e.,

$$\left(\frac{\theta}{\varphi\varrho^{1-\beta}}\right)^{1/(1-\alpha)}\frac{Z}{l} < N_t < \frac{Z}{\varrho l}. \tag{5.25}$$

Then, the transition from hunting-gathering to agriculture begins. We can substitute (5.13) into (5.20) to derive the population growth rate as

$$\frac{\Delta N_t}{N_t} = \frac{\gamma}{\rho}\varphi\varrho^{1-\beta}l - 1 > 0, \tag{5.26}$$

which is positive if and only if the transition to agriculture occurs (i.e., $\gamma\varphi\varrho^{1-\beta}l > \rho$) and implies that population N_t increases over time during the gradual transition from hunting-gathering to agriculture.

5.2.4   Stage 3: Complete transition to agriculture

Given (5.26), the level of population N_t eventually crosses the second threshold, i.e.,

$$N_t > \frac{Z}{\varrho l}. \tag{5.27}$$

At this stage, we can substitute (5.14) into (5.20) to derive the growth rate of the population as

$$\frac{\Delta N_t}{N_t} = \frac{\gamma}{\rho}\varphi l^{\beta}\left(\frac{Z}{N_t}\right)^{1-\beta} - 1, \tag{5.28}$$

which yields a steady-state level of population in agriculture as

$$N_A^* = \left(\frac{\gamma}{\rho} \varphi l^\beta \right)^{1/(1-\beta)} Z. \tag{5.29}$$

In this case, the economy would remain in an agricultural Malthusian trap indefinitely. Substituting (5.29) into (5.14) yields $y^* = f^* = \rho/\gamma$, which is once again increasing in fertility cost ρ and decreasing in the degree γ of fertility preference but independent of agricultural productivity φ and land Z. In this agricultural Malthusian trap, higher agricultural productivity φ and more land Z increase the steady-state level of population N_A^* but not the per capita level of farming output f^* in the long run.

5.2.5   Dynamics of population growth

If the population manages to evolve from hunting-gathering to agriculture, the dynamics of the population growth rate can be summarized as follows:

$$\frac{\Delta N_t}{N_t} = \frac{\gamma}{\rho}(h_t + f_t) - 1$$

$$= \begin{cases} \frac{\gamma}{\rho}\theta l^\alpha \left(\frac{Z}{N_t} \right)^{1-\alpha} - 1 & \text{for } N_t < \left(\frac{\theta}{\varphi \varrho^{1-\beta}} \right)^{1/(1-\alpha)} \frac{Z}{l} \\ \frac{\gamma}{\rho}\varphi \varrho^{1-\beta} l - 1 & \text{for } \left(\frac{\theta}{\varphi \varrho^{1-\beta}} \right)^{1/(1-\alpha)} \frac{Z}{l} < N_t < \frac{Z}{\varrho l} \\ \frac{\gamma}{\rho}\varphi l^\beta \left(\frac{Z}{N_t} \right)^{1-\beta} - 1 & \text{for } N_t > \frac{Z}{\varrho l} \end{cases}.$$

$$\tag{5.30}$$

Figure 5.2 plots the population growth rate $\Delta N_t/N_t$ for the following two scenarios: (a) the population does not experience the transition to agriculture and converges to a hunting-gathering Malthusian trap, as in Section 5.2.1; and (b) the population evolves from hunter-gatherers to an agricultural society and converges to an agricultural Malthusian trap, as in Section 5.2.4.

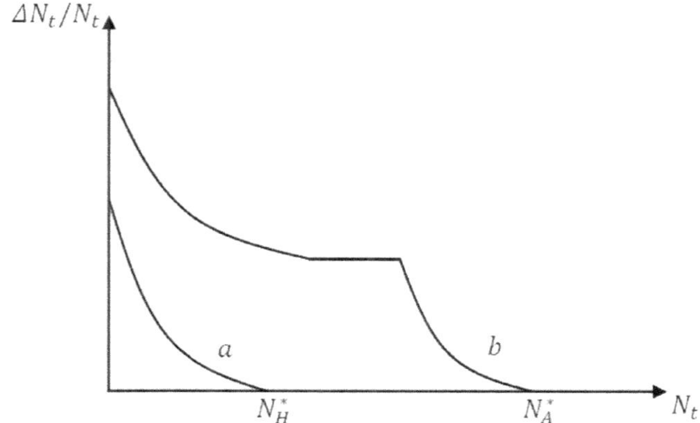

Figure 5.2. Dynamics of population growth.

5.3 Summary and Discussion

In this chapter, we have extended the Malthusian growth model to capture the economic evolution of human society from hunting-gathering to agriculture. We show that under endogenous population growth in a Malthusian environment, the Neolithic Revolution is not inevitable. If the population size fails to reach the agricultural threshold, then the human population remains as hunter-gatherers. Only if the population size reaches the agricultural threshold does an agricultural society emerge.

Our extended Malthusian growth model identifies several potential causes for the Neolithic Revolution: a high level of agricultural productivity, a low cost of fertility, and a strong preference for fertility. An implication is that the transitions to agriculture in different parts of the world (such as Central Mexico, China, the Middle East, and Sub-Saharan Africa) at different time periods could have been triggered by different reasons despite the fact that they all experienced the transition from hunting-gathering to agriculture.[10]

---

[10] A recent study by Matranga (2024) shows that seasonal fluctuations in hunting-gathering output amplified by climatic variation made agriculture a more attractive choice of food production, which can also be captured in our Malthusian

Furthermore, the theoretical result that a high level of agricultural productivity triggers the Neolithic Revolution is supported by both empirical evidence and archeological evidence.[11]

In agricultural settlements, civilizations gradually emerged, first in Mesopotamia (which is in present-day Iraq) and subsequently in ancient Egypt, China, and the Indus Valley. Political organization of early agricultural settlements was in the form of chiefdoms, which were based on kinship and gradually developed into political states.[12] In the following chapter, we explore the next stage of the political evolution of human society from multiple competing states to a unified empire.

---

framework by allowing for uncertainty in hunting-gathering productivity, reducing the expected utility of hunting-gathering consumption.

[11]See Olsson (2001), Olsson and Hibbs (2005), Ashraf and Galor (2011), Ang (2015), and Chu and Xu (2024).

[12]For example, in China, Taosi (2300 BC–1900 BC) was a chiefdom in the late Neolithic Age that immediately preceded the Erlitou culture (1900 BC–1500 BC) in the early Bronze Age. Erlitou is often viewed as an early state and the site of the Xia dynasty in ancient China.

Chapter 6

From Political Fragmentation to a Unified Empire

The previous chapter explores how human society evolves from hunting-gathering to agriculture. Agricultural settlements gave rise to civilizations and political states. In this chapter, we explore how agricultural settlements evolve from multiple competing states to a unified empire. Historically, ancient China had a tendency toward a unified empire, whereas Europe had a tendency toward political fragmentation. However, there was also an extended period of political fragmentation in ancient China before a unified empire became the norm with the establishment of the Qin dynasty in 221 BC, which is often known as the first dynasty of Imperial China.[1] During the Warring States period from 481 BC to 221 BC, there were seven major states (including the Qin state) and many minor states competing with each other. Therefore, an interesting question is why ancient China evolved from multiple states to a unified empire, whereas medieval Europe largely maintained its political fragmentation. In other words, "where did this political fragmentation come from?

---

[1]The Shang dynasty (1600–1045 BC) is the first dynasty with evidence of writing in ancient China. It is followed by the Western Zhou (1045–771 BC) and the Spring and Autumn period (770–481 BC). Neither the Shang dynasty nor the Zhou dynasty is a unified empire.

57

Why was Europe decentralised and characterised by competition among relatively small powers, while extensive regions of Asia were controlled by monolithic mega-empires?"[2]

This chapter develops a Malthusian growth model with multiple states to explore interstate competition and the endogenous evolution of human society from political fragmentation to a unified empire.[3] Our model features agricultural states with citizens and rulers in a Malthusian environment in which the population size of a state is determined by the amount of land it occupies. We adopt a conflict success function for the division of land between competing states, and the share of land occupied by each state is an increasing function in its share of the total population. Therefore, the expansion of one state may come at the expense of another state, depending on the intensity of interstate competition captured by the elasticity of the land ratio with respect to the ratio of population between states. If this elasticity is less than unity, then multiple states coexist in the steady-state equilibrium. However, if this elasticity is equal to unity, then interstate competition is so strong that only one state (i.e., an empire) survives in the long run. Which state becomes the unified empire depends on population growth, which is increasing in the state's level of agricultural productivity[4] and the degree of its citizens' fertility preference but decreasing in the degree of the rulers' preference for rent-seeking Leviathan taxation.[5]

---

[2]Galor (2022, p. 184).

[3]The model in this chapter is a simplified version of the one in Chu *et al.* (2024b). See also Chaudhry and Garner (2006), Karayalcin (2008), Chu (2010), and Lagerlof (2014) for other growth-theoretic studies on interstate competition and economic growth.

[4]Willmott (1989) and Bello (2020) argue that the irrigation system in the Qin state (e.g., the Dujiangyan and Zhengguo Canal built in 256 BC and 246 BC, respectively) improved the state's agricultural productivity and provided the foundation for its unification of China.

[5]Shang Yang's political and economic reforms also laid the foundation for Qin's unification of China by weakening the extractive power of landed aristocrats; see Kiser and Cai (2003).

6.1 A Malthusian Model with Interstate Competition

To explore interstate competition, we extend the Malthusian growth model by introducing multiple states indexed by superscript $i \in \{1, \ldots, m\}$. As in Chapter 4, competition over land is captured by a conflict success function. Furthermore, there are citizens and rulers in each state. Unlike the egalitarian hunting-gathering tribes, a ruling class emerges in an agricultural society. Citizens engage in agricultural production, whereas rulers impose a tax on the agricultural output of citizens and consume the tax revenue.

6.1.1 Agricultural production

Farming requires both labor and land. In state i, the farming output of a citizen at time t is

$$ y_t^i = \varphi^i (l^i)^\beta (z_t^i)^{1-\beta} = \varphi^i (l^i)^\beta \left(\frac{Z_t^i}{N_t^i} \right)^{1-\beta}, \tag{6.1} $$

where $\varphi^i > 0$ measures agricultural productivity in state i and $\beta \in (0, 1)$ measures labor intensity in agriculture, which is assumed to be the same across states for simplicity. z_t^i is the amount of land distributed to the citizen. The amount of land occupied by state i is Z_t^i and is equally distributed to its citizens such that $z_t^i = Z_t^i/N_t^i$, where N_t^i is the number of adult citizens in state i at time t.

6.1.2 Endogenous fertility

In state i, there are N_t^i adult citizens at time t. As before, each agent lives for two periods. An adult citizen in state i at time t has the following utility function:

$$ u_t^i = (1 - \gamma^i) \ln c_t^i + \gamma^i \ln n_t^i, \tag{6.2} $$

where $\gamma^i \in (0, 1)$ measures the degree of preference for fertility n_t^i, which denotes the citizen's number of children. There is a cost of raising children, ρn_t^i, where $\rho > 0$ determines the fertility cost.[6] As a result, the citizen's level of consumption c_t^i net of the fertility cost is given by

$$c_t^i = (1 - \tau_t^i)y_t^i - \rho n_t^i, \tag{6.3}$$

where $\tau_t^i \in (0,1)$ is the tax rate on farming output imposed by the rulers in state i. Substituting (6.1) and (6.3) into (6.2), we derive the utility-maximizing level of fertility as

$$n_t^i = \frac{\gamma^i}{\rho}(1 - \tau_t^i)y_t^i, \tag{6.4}$$

and the utility-maximizing level of consumption as

$$c_t^i = (1 - \gamma^i)(1 - \tau_t^i)y_t^i. \tag{6.5}$$

Each adult citizen in state i has n_t^i children, and the number of adult citizens at time t is N_t^i, which we simply refer to as the population size. Then, the law of motion for the population size in state i is

$$N_{t+1}^i = n_t^i N_t^i = \frac{\gamma^i}{\rho}(1 - \tau_t^i)y_t^i N_t^i, \tag{6.6}$$

and the population growth rate in state i is

$$\frac{\Delta N_t^i}{N_t^i} = \frac{\gamma^i}{\rho}(1 - \tau_t^i)y_t^i - 1, \tag{6.7}$$

which is increasing in the after-tax agricultural output $(1 - \tau_t^i)y_t^i$ and the fertility preference γ^i of citizens in state i.

6.1.3   Rulers

Each state i is governed by a group of rulers. The objective function of the generation of rulers at time t is

$$U_t^i = \lambda^i \ln T_t^i + (1 - \lambda^i) \ln N_{t+1}^i, \tag{6.8}$$

where the parameter $\lambda^i \in (0,1)$ measures the degree of the rulers' preference for rent-seeking Leviathan taxation T_t^i. The tax revenue

---

[6]Allowing the fertility cost ρ to vary across states would not change our results.

that the rulers collect for their own consumption is[7]

$$T_t^i = \tau_t^i y_t^i N_t^i. \tag{6.9}$$

Although the rulers want to collect as much tax revenue as possible, they also care about the future population size N_{t+1}^i of their state. Taking N_t^i as given, the rulers choose τ_t^i to maximize U_t^i. Substituting (6.1), (6.6), and (6.9) into (6.8), we derive the tax rate chosen by the rulers as

$$\tau_t^i = \lambda^i, \tag{6.10}$$

which is increasing in the degree of their preference for rent-seeking taxation.

6.1.4 Land competition

We consider the conflict success function for the division of land between competing states. Specifically, the amount of land occupied by state $i \in \{1, \ldots, m\}$ is specified as follows[8]:

$$Z_t^i = \frac{(N_t^i)^\phi}{\sum_{j=1}^m (N_t^j)^\phi} Z, \tag{6.11}$$

where $Z > 0$ is the total amount of land. If $\phi = 0$, then the amount of land is equally divided between all states, such that $Z_t^i = Z/m$, for all $i \in \{1, \ldots, m\}$. As ϕ increases, the ratio of land becomes more sensitive to the population ratio:

$$\frac{Z_t^i}{Z_t^j} = \left(\frac{N_t^i}{N_t^j} \right)^\phi, \tag{6.12}$$

---

[7]Our results are robust to T_t^i being used for providing a utility-enhancing public good to citizens, so long as this public good is separable in their utility function u_t^i.

[8]Chu *et al.* (2024b) allow for asymmetric military power μ^i across states by generalizing (6.11) to $Z_t^i = \mu^i (N_t^i)^\phi Z / \sum_{j=1}^m \mu^j (N_t^j)^\phi$. In Section 6.2.4, we discuss how one of our results changes in this case.

which shows that ϕ parameterizes the elasticity of the land ratio with respect to the ratio of population between states. This crucial parameter determines whether a unified empire emerges or not.

6.2   From Political Fragmentation to a Unified Empire

Substituting (6.11) into (6.1), we reexpress the population growth rate of state i in (6.7) as

$$\frac{\Delta N_t^i}{N_t^i} = \frac{\gamma^i}{\rho}(1 - \lambda^i)\varphi^i(l^i)^\beta \left[\frac{(N_t^i)^\phi}{\sum_{j=1}^m (N_t^j)^\phi} \frac{Z}{N_t^i} \right]^{1-\beta} - 1. \tag{6.13}$$

For a given level of population across states, the transitional growth rate of population in state i at time t is increasing in the state's level of agricultural productivity φ^i and the degree of its citizens' fertility preference γ^i but decreasing in the rulers' preference λ^i for rent-seeking taxation, regardless of the value of the decisiveness parameter ϕ. However, the long-run population dynamics differs drastically for different values of $\phi \in [0, 1]$. In the following sections, we consider the following three scenarios: $\phi = 0$, $\phi \in (0, 1)$, and $\phi = 1$.

6.2.1   No competition between states

The first case that we consider is $\phi = 0$. In this case, the population dynamics of the m states in (6.13) is independent of each other and simplifies to

$$\frac{\Delta N_t^i}{N_t^i} = \frac{\gamma^i}{\rho}(1 - \lambda^i)\varphi^i(l^i)^\beta \left(\frac{Z}{mN_t^i} \right)^{1-\beta} - 1, \tag{6.14}$$

in which the amount of land occupied by each state is simply $Z_t^i = Z/m$. Therefore, there is no dynamics in the relative land share across states, and the model features only the usual Malthusian population dynamics within each state.

Figure 6.1 shows that given any initial level of population N_0^i in state i, the population size N_t^i converges to a unique and stable

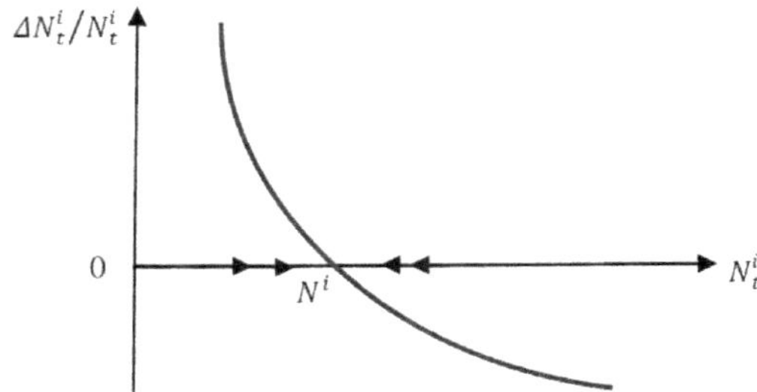

Figure 6.1. Phase diagram for $\phi = 0$.

steady state:

$$N^i = \left[\frac{\gamma^i(1 - \lambda^i)\varphi^i(l^i)^\beta}{\rho}\right]^{1/(1-\beta)} \frac{Z}{m}, \qquad (6.15)$$

which shows that the steady-state population level N^i is increasing in the amount of land in each state Z/m and decreasing in the fertility cost ρ. Also, N^i is an increasing function in a state-specific composite parameter $\gamma^i(1 - \lambda^i)\varphi^i(l^i)^\beta$, which in turn is increasing in the state's level of agricultural productivity φ^i and the degree of its citizens' fertility preference γ^i but decreasing in the rulers' preference λ^i for rent-seeking taxation.

6.2.2 Interstate competition and political fragmentation

The second case that we consider is $\phi \in (0, 1)$. In this case, the population dynamics of the m states in (6.13) depends on each other. Setting $\Delta N_t^i = 0$ in (6.13) yields

$$N^i = \left[\frac{\gamma^i(1 - \lambda^i)\varphi^i(l^i)^\beta}{\rho}\right]^{1/(1-\beta)} \left[\sum_{j=1}^{m}\left(\frac{N^j}{N^i}\right)^\phi\right]^{-1} Z, \qquad (6.16)$$

where the population ratio between any two states is given by

$$\frac{N^i}{N^j} = \left[\frac{\gamma^i(1 - \lambda^i)\varphi^i(l^i)^\beta}{\gamma^j(1 - \lambda^j)\varphi^j(l^j)^\beta}\right]^{1/[(1-\beta)(1-\phi)]}, \qquad (6.17)$$

which also determines the relative land share as $Z_t^i/Z_t^j = (N_t^i/N_t^j)^\phi$ from (6.12). Therefore, the dynamics in the relative land share across states interact with the Malthusian population dynamics within each state. As state i's population size increases relative to another state, state i can also capture some of its land and sustain an even larger population size relative to the other state.

Given an initial population level N_0^i in state $i \in \{1, \ldots, m\}$, N_t^i converges to the unique and stable steady state N^i in (6.16). For $m = 2$, the phase diagram is given in Figure 6.2. For $m > 2$, Chu *et al.* (2024b) show that the dynamics is also stable. As before, the steady-state population size N^i is increasing in the total amount of land Z and decreasing in the fertility cost ρ. Furthermore, N^i is an increasing function of the state-specific composite parameter $\gamma^i(1 - \lambda^i)\varphi^i(l^i)^\beta$, as before, but is now a decreasing function of the composite parameters $\gamma^j(1 - \lambda^j)\varphi^j(l^j)^\beta$ of other states $j \neq i$. In other words, due to interstate competition, the steady-state population size N^i in state i is decreasing in the other states' level of agricultural productivity φ^j and the degree of their citizens' fertility preference γ^j but increasing in the other state rulers' preference λ^j for rent-seeking taxation. More importantly, all m states continue to coexist at the steady state under $\phi \in (0, 1)$ despite the presence of interstate competition.

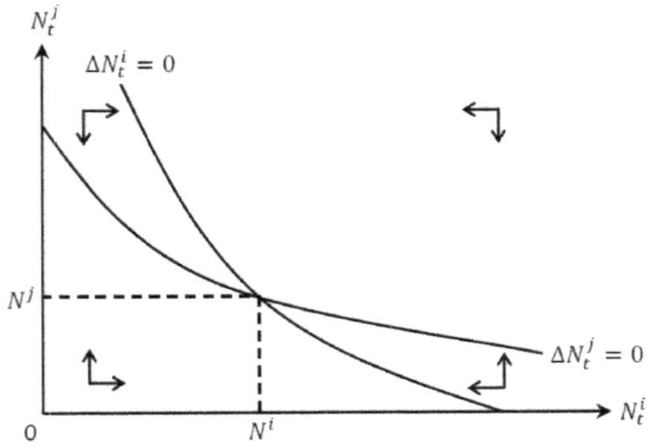

Figure 6.2.   Phase diagram for $\phi \in (0, 1)$.

6.2.3 Unified empire and political unification

The third case that we consider is $\phi = 1$. In this case, (6.13) simplifies to

$$\frac{\Delta N_t^i}{N_t^i} = \frac{\gamma^i}{\rho}(1 - \lambda^i)\varphi^i(l^i)^\beta \left(\frac{Z}{N_t}\right)^{1-\beta} - 1, \qquad (6.18)$$

in which the land share of state i is simply $Z_t^i/Z = N_t^i/N_t$ from (6.11), where $N_t \equiv \sum_{i=1}^m N_t^i$. Therefore, the dynamics in the relative land share across states becomes the same as the dynamics in the population share across states, such that population growth in all states depends on the total amount of land per capita (i.e., Z/N_t).

Suppose we assume $\gamma^i(1 - \lambda^i)\varphi^i(l^i)^\beta > \gamma^j(1 - \lambda^j)\varphi^j(l^j)^\beta$ for all $j \neq i$. Then, state i has the highest population growth rate among all the states. In the long run, given any initial population size N_0^j across states $j \in \{1, \ldots, m\}$, the population sizes N_t^j for all $j \neq i$ converge to 0, whereas N_t^i converges to

$$N^i = \left[\frac{\gamma^i(1 - \lambda^i)\varphi^i(l^i)^\beta}{\rho}\right]^{1/(1-\beta)} Z, \qquad (6.19)$$

which, as before, is increasing in the amount of land Z and decreasing in the fertility cost ρ. For $m = 2$, the phase diagram is given in Figure 6.3. For $m > 2$, Chu *et al.* (2024b) show that only the state that has the largest state-specific composite parameter $\gamma^i(1 - \lambda^i)\varphi^i(l^i)^\beta$ emerges as the empire in the long run and all other states eventually collapse. Furthermore, the steady-state equilibrium size of this empire is increasing in the level of agricultural productivity φ^i and the citizens' fertility preference γ^i but decreasing in the rulers' preference λ^i for rent-seeking taxation.

6.2.4 Population size under different political regimes

Interestingly, the unified empire achieves a larger steady-state population size than the total population size of multiple states. In an agricultural economy, interstate competition favors the state with the

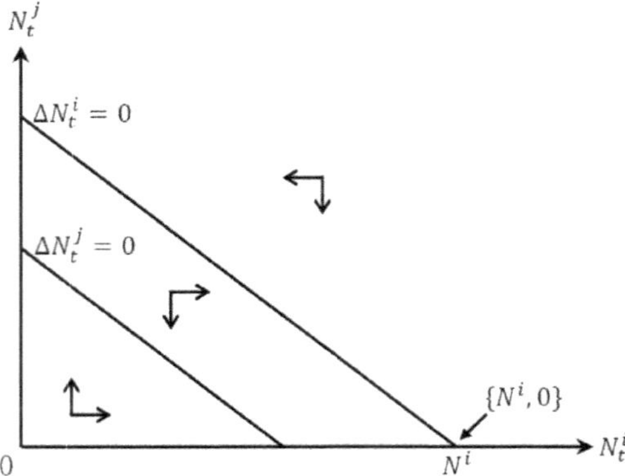

Figure 6.3. Phase diagram for $\phi = 1$.

highest population growth. As a result, the unified empire's steady-state population size N^i in (6.19) is greater than $\sum_{i=1}^{m} N^i$ in (6.15) or (6.16) when multiple states coexist in the long run.[9]

To see this result, we denote $\Omega^i \equiv \gamma^i(1 - \lambda^i)\varphi^i(l^i)^\beta$ as the state-specific composite parameter. Recall that the unified empire is the state with the largest Ω^i, which we now denote as $\Omega^{\max}$, and we also denote N^i in (6.19) as $N^{\max}$. Then, the inequality $N^{\max} > \sum_{i=1}^{m} N^i$ in (6.15) or (6.16) can be reexpressed as

$$(\Omega^{\max})^{1/(1-\beta)} > \sum_{i=1}^{m} \omega^i (\Omega^i)^{1/(1-\beta)} > \frac{1}{m} \sum_{i=1}^{m} (\Omega^i)^{1/(1-\beta)}, \qquad (6.20)$$

where the weight is defined as $\omega^i \equiv (\Omega^i)^{\phi/[(1-\beta)(1-\phi)]} / \sum_{j=1}^{m} (\Omega^j)^{\phi/[(1-\beta)(1-\phi)]}$. Equation (6.20) holds because $(\Omega^{\max})^{1/(1-\beta)}$ is greater than both the weighted average of $(\Omega^i)^{1/(1-\beta)}$ in (6.16) and the unweighted average of $(\Omega^i)^{1/(1-\beta)}$ in (6.15). It also shows that the total population size under multiple states is larger with interstate

---

[9]Chu *et al.* (2024b) show that if the unified empire achieves its empire formation solely via military superiority (e.g., the Mongol Empire), then this result may not hold because military power only contributes to population growth via the competition of resources but does not improve the efficiency of the conversion of natural resources to population growth.

competition than without interstate competition because the weight ω^i is increasing in Ω^i. Intuitively, with interstate competition, countries with larger Ω^i have larger populations and capture more land, which in turn can support an even larger population size. Therefore, in an agricultural economy, interstate competition is beneficial to population growth in the long run.

6.3 Summary and Discussion

In this chapter, we have developed an agricultural Malthusian growth model with interstate competition and derived an endogenous political evolution of human society from multiple states to a unified empire. Whether political fragmentation or a unified empire emerges in the long run depends on the elasticity of the land ratio with respect to the ratio of population between states. This parameter captures the intensity of interstate competition, which in turn can be determined by more fundamental causes such as geographic barriers. For example, using a quantitative spatial model, Fernandez-Villaverde *et al.* (2023) provide empirical support for the importance of the fractured-land hypothesis[10] on the origins of political fragmentation in Europe and political unification in China. The idea is that the European landscape fractured by high mountains led to a low intensity of interstate competition, which can be captured by a low elasticity of the land ratio with respect to the ratio of population between states in our model. In contrast, the lack of such high mountains in the Chinese landscape gave rise to a high intensity of interstate competition and a tendency toward political unification in ancient China.

Our growth-theoretic analysis also suggests that which state becomes the unified empire depends on factors such as the productivity of agricultural production and the rent-seeking taxation of rulers.

---

[10]See Diamond (1997), who popularized this hypothesis.

In the case of the Qin state in ancient China, it is indeed often argued that its irrigation system, which improved agricultural productivity,[11] and its political and economic reforms, which limited the extractive power of landed aristocrats,[12] were partly responsible for its unification of China.[13] In the following chapter, we explore the next transition of human society from an agricultural economy to an industrial economy.

---

[11]See, for example, Willmott (1989) and Bello (2020).

[12]See, for example, Kiser and Cai (2003).

[13]After the Qin unification, Imperial China remained a unified empire most of the time from the Han dynasty (202 BC–AD 220) to the Qing dynasty (1636–1912), with some relatively brief periods of political fragmentation in between.

Part III
Industrial Era

Chapter 7

The Industrial Revolution

After the Neolithic Revolution, human society remained in an agricultural economy for over 10,000 years. However, in the late 18th and early 19th centuries, the Industrial Revolution (the transition from agriculture to industrial production that began with new modes of production, such as the factory, mass production, and mechanization, which greatly improved labor productivity) took place in Britain and then in continental Europe and the United States. "The past two hundred years, therefore, have been revolutionary: living standards have taken an unprecedented leap forward by every conceivable measure."[1] For example, per capita income in Western Europe was roughly \$400 in 1000, \$1000 in 1700, and \$1200 in 1820.[2] Then, it increased drastically to about \$20,000 in 2000. Was this industrial transition of human society inevitable? If not, what are the different conditions that could have potentially made the industrial transition more or less likely to occur?

In this chapter, we extend the Malthusian growth model to capture the economic evolution of human society from an agricultural economy to an industrial economy.[3] The extended Malthusian growth

---

[1]Galor (2022, p. 122).

[2]In constant 1990 international \$. Data source: Maddison (2007).

[3]This chapter is based on Chu and Xu (2024). See Galor (2005, 2011) and Doepke (2008) for surveys of growth-theoretic studies on industrial takeoff.

model features agricultural production, which exhibits decreasing returns to scale in labor, and industrial production, which exhibits increasing returns to scale in labor. Human society evolves from agricultural production to industrial production as the size of the population grows. Given the Malthusian environment, the population may stop growing and never reach the industrial threshold under endogenous population growth. If the population size fails to reach this threshold, then the population remains in an agricultural Malthusian trap and does not experience industrialization. Here, the importance of the population size on industrialization is due to its increasing returns to scale (i.e., having a large enough market to cover the fixed costs associated with industrial production), as given by Murphy *et al.* (1989). If the population reaches the industrial threshold, then an industrial economy emerges and exhibits positive population growth in the long run.

We find that industrialization is influenced by the same conditions as the Neolithic Revolution in Chapter 5 (namely, a high level of agricultural productivity, a low cost of fertility, and a strong preference for fertility) and also other conditions: a high level of industrial productivity and a low fixed cost of industrial production. For example, the invention of the steam engine improved industrial productivity and contributed to the industrialization of the British economy.[4] Furthermore, a high level of agricultural productivity not only triggered the Neolithic Revolution but also contributed to the subsequent industrialization. Chu and Xu (2024) use cross-country data to examine this theoretical result. They follow previous empirical studies, such as those by Olsson and Hibbs (2005), Ashraf and Galor (2011), and Ang (2015), to consider an index of biogeographic conditions as an instrument for the timing of transition to agriculture

---

[4]The steam engine is a classic example of general-purpose technologies; see Helpman (2003) for a book treatment on general-purpose technologies and economic growth.

and find that an earlier transition to agriculture (driven by higher agricultural productivity) indeed has a positive effect on the degree of industrialization in modern times.

7.1 A Static Model of Economic Evolution

We extend the Malthusian growth model in Chapter 5 to introduce an industrial economy as the third stage of economic evolution. As before, we first present a static version of the model with an exogenous level of population before extending the model to a dynamic version with endogenous population growth. Initially, human society is in an agricultural economy. Then, an industrial economy emerges. The population consists of N identical agents.[5] Each agent is endowed with l units of labor, which can be allocated to farming l_F or industrial production l_X. Therefore, the labor constraint faced by each agent is

$$l_F + l_X = l. \tag{7.1}$$

There is also a fixed amount of agricultural land Z for farming.[6]

7.1.1 Agricultural production

Farming requires both labor and land. The farming production of an agent, who devotes l_F units of labor to farming, is

$$f = \varphi(l_F)^\beta z^{1-\beta}, \tag{7.2}$$

where the parameters $\varphi > 0$ and $\beta \in (0,1)$ measure, respectively, the productivity and labor intensity in agriculture. z is the amount

---

[5]In this chapter, we use N to denote the exogenous level of population in the static model and N^* to denote the steady-state level of population in the dynamic model.

[6]For simplicity, we assume the degree of land intensity in industrial production to be negligible.

of land used by the agent. As in Chapter 5, we assume a fixed ratio ϱ of land to farming labor given by

$$z = \varrho l_F \tag{7.3}$$

when agricultural land is not scarce (i.e., $\varrho \bar{l}_F N < Z$); in this case, $f = \varphi \varrho^{1-\beta} l_F$. When agricultural land becomes scarce, it is equally divided between agents; i.e.,

$$z = Z/N. \tag{7.4}$$

7.1.2　Industrial production

As given by Murphy *et al.* (1989), the operation of industrial production requires a fixed cost $\delta > 0$ (e.g., the cost of building a steam engine) under which total industrial output is given by

$$X = A(\bar{l}_X N - \delta), \tag{7.5}$$

where $\bar{l}_X N$ is the total amount of labor devoted to industrial production and the parameter $A > 0$ determines the level of industrial productivity. The fixed cost is shared by all agents when the industrial economy operates. Then, the output of industrial production received by an agent, who devotes l_X units of labor, is

$$x = A\left(l_X - \frac{\delta}{N}\right). \tag{7.6}$$

Due to the fixed cost δ, the industrial market would not operate (despite the potentially higher level of industrial productivity A) unless the population size N is sufficiently large.

7.1.3　From agriculture to industrialization

We now explore the evolution of the economy. The society is initially in an agricultural economy before an industrial economy emerges. Each agent maximizes consumption c, given by

$$c = y = x + f, \tag{7.7}$$

where y is total output per capita. Here, we make a simplifying assumption that there is perfect substitutability between farming production f and industrial production x in the consumption of agents. This assumption helps to keep our analysis tractable and is not entirely unrealistic because industrial production includes food production.

7.1.4 Agricultural economy

At this stage of the economy, an industrial market still does not emerge because the population size is insufficient to cover the fixed cost δ. This threshold value of N is implicitly determined by the following equality:

$$\varphi l^{\beta}\left(\frac{Z}{N}\right)^{1-\beta} = A\left(l - \frac{\delta}{N}\right), \tag{7.8}$$

in which the left-hand side is farming output per capita when $l_F = l$ and decreasing in N, whereas the right-hand side is industrial output per capita when $l_X = l$ and increasing in N. Therefore, there exists a unique cutoff value of N for the emergence of an industrial economy, which is denoted as N_I and has the following comparative statics:

$$N_I(\underset{+}{\varphi}, \underset{+}{Z}, \underset{+}{\delta}, \underset{-}{A}, \underset{-}{l}). \tag{7.9}$$

For example, this implies that, by making agriculture more productive, higher agricultural productivity φ delays industrialization, which contradicts the evidence discussed in the seminal study by Nurkse (1953) and in many subsequent studies.[7] As we will show, this counterfactual result will be overturned under endogenous population growth.

In summary, if the following inequality holds:

$$N < N_I, \tag{7.10}$$

---

[7]According to Nurkse (1953), technological improvements that raised agricultural productivity helped to release labor from agriculture to industrial production and were crucial for the Industrial Revolution. See also Chu *et al.* (2022c) and the studies discussed there.

then the agents would be better off allocating all their labor to farming (i.e., $l_F = l$). In this case, the level of output per capita is given by[8]

$$y = f = \varphi l^{\beta} \left(\frac{Z}{N} \right)^{1-\beta}, \tag{7.11}$$

which is increasing in agricultural productivity φ, labor supply l, and the amount of land Z but decreasing in the population size N due to the decreasing returns to labor in farming when agricultural land is scarce.

7.1.5 Industrial economy

If $N > N_I$, then the transition from agriculture to an industrial economy occurs. In this case, the level of output per capita is given by

$$y = x = A \left(l - \frac{\delta}{N} \right), \tag{7.12}$$

which is increasing in industrial productivity A, labor supply l, and population size N but decreasing in the fixed cost δ of industrial production. Equation (7.12) is obtained by setting $l_X = l$ in (7.6). When the population size is sufficiently large, the agents would immediately allocate all their labor to industrial production given the following parameter assumption: $A > \varphi \varrho^{1-\beta}$. In this case, the marginal product of industrial labor is greater than the marginal product of agricultural labor, i.e.,

$$A > \varphi \varrho^{1-\beta} > \varphi (l_F)^{\beta-1} \left(\frac{Z}{N} \right)^{1-\beta} > \beta \varphi (l_F)^{\beta-1} \left(\frac{Z}{N} \right)^{1-\beta}$$

for $l_F > Z/(\varrho N)$. For $l_F < Z/(\varrho N)$, the marginal product of agricultural labor is simply $\varphi \varrho^{1-\beta} < A$.

---

[8]Here, we assume $N > Z/(\varrho l)$. For the case of $N < Z/(\varrho l)$, see Chapter 5.

7.1.6 Consumption at different stages

In this section, we summarize the level of consumption per capita at different levels of population as follows:

$$c = y = \begin{cases} f = \varphi l^{\beta} \left(\dfrac{Z}{N}\right)^{1-\beta} & \text{for } N < N_I \\[2ex] x = A\left(l - \dfrac{\delta}{N}\right) & \text{for } N > N_I \end{cases} \qquad (7.13)$$

Equation (7.13) presents the level of per capita consumption c as population N increases. In summary, consumption c is initially falling due to the decreasing returns to labor in agriculture. When the industrial economy emerges, consumption c becomes rising (capturing a rising standard of living) due to the increasing returns to scale in the presence of a fixed cost of industrial production and converges toward a steady-state level, given by $y = x = Al$ as $N \to \infty$.

7.2 A Dynamic Model with Endogenous Population Growth

The previous section presents a static model with an exogenous level of population. This section extends the model into a dynamic setting with endogenous population growth. As in previous chapters, each agent lives for two periods, and each adult agent at time t has the following utility function:

$$u_t = (1 - \gamma) \ln c_t + \gamma \ln n_t, \qquad (7.14)$$

where $\gamma \in (0, 1)$ measures the preference for fertility and n_t is the agent's number of children. Raising children is costly, and the level of consumption net of the fertility cost is given by

$$c_t = y_t - \rho n_t, \qquad (7.15)$$

where $\rho > 0$ determines the cost of fertility. Substituting (7.15) into (7.14), we derive the utility-maximizing level of fertility n_t as

$$n_t = \frac{\gamma}{\rho} y_t \tag{7.16}$$

and $c_t = (1 - \gamma)y_t$, in which the agent maximizes $y_t = x_t + f_t$ as in the previous section.

Each adult agent has n_t children, and the number of adult agents at time t is N_t. Therefore, the law of motion for the adult population size is given by

$$N_{t+1} = n_t N_t = \frac{\gamma}{\rho} y_t N_t, \tag{7.17}$$

and the adult population growth rate at time t is

$$\frac{\Delta N_t}{N_t} = \frac{\gamma}{\rho} y_t - 1 = \frac{\gamma}{\rho}(x_t + f_t) - 1, \tag{7.18}$$

which will be referred to as the population growth rate. In the following, we use the information from the previous section to derive the population dynamics.

7.2.1　Agricultural economy

At this stage, the level of population N_t is below the industrial threshold N_I, which is implicitly given in (7.8) and (7.9). We can substitute (7.11) into (7.18) to derive the growth rate of the population as

$$\frac{\Delta N_t}{N_t} = \frac{\gamma}{\rho} \varphi l^\beta \left(\frac{Z}{N_t}\right)^{1-\beta} - 1, \tag{7.19}$$

which yields a steady-state level of population in agriculture as

$$N_A^* = \left(\frac{\gamma}{\rho} \varphi l^\beta\right)^{1/(1-\beta)} Z. \tag{7.20}$$

If N_t reaches N_A^* before reaching N_I, then the population would remain as an agricultural society indefinitely. Substituting (7.20) into (7.11) yields $y^* = f^* = \rho/\gamma$, which is once again increasing in fertility cost ρ and decreasing in the degree γ of fertility preference but independent of agricultural productivity φ and land Z. In other words, the population is now in an agricultural Malthusian trap, in which higher agricultural productivity φ and more land Z increase the steady-state level of population N_A^* but not the per capita level of farming output f^* in the long run.

7.2.2 Industrial economy

If the level of population N_t manages to cross the industrial threshold N_I, then an industrial economy emerges. In this case, we can substitute (7.12) into (7.18) to derive the population growth rate as

$$\frac{\Delta N_t}{N_t} = \frac{\gamma A}{\rho}\left(l - \frac{\delta}{N_t}\right) - 1, \qquad (7.21)$$

which is increasing in N_t. Setting $\Delta N_t/N_t = 0$ in (7.21) yields the following (unstable) steady-state level:

$$N_I^* = \frac{\delta}{l - \rho/(\gamma A)}, \qquad (7.22)$$

above which the population grows over time during the industrial era.

Figure 7.1 shows that if and only if $N_A^* > N_I^*$, then N_t would reach the industrial threshold N_I and trigger the emergence of an

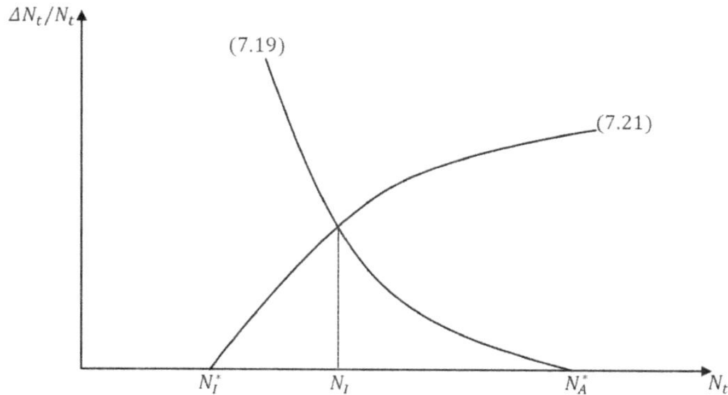

Figure 7.1. Industrial threshold.

industrial economy. When $N_t > N_I$, the per capita level of output y_t is higher under industrial production than under agricultural production. From (7.20) and (7.22), the inequality $N_A^* > N_I^*$ is equivalent to

$$\left(l - \frac{\rho}{\gamma A}\right)\left(\frac{\gamma}{\rho}\varphi l^\beta\right)^{1/(1-\beta)} \frac{Z}{\delta} > 1. \tag{7.23}$$

Therefore, the transition from an agricultural economy to an industrial economy occurs under the following conditions: a low fertility cost ρ, a strong fertility preference γ, a high level of agricultural productivity φ, a high level of labor supply l, a large amount of land Z, a high level of industrial productivity A, and a low fixed cost δ of industrial production.

As before, a strong fertility preference γ and a low fertility cost ρ give rise to a higher level of population and make it more likely for the population to cross the threshold N_I for the emergence of an industrial economy, but they also reduce steady-state farming output per capita $y^* = f^* = \rho/\gamma$ in case the population remains in an agricultural Malthusian trap. Interestingly, unlike the case of exogenous population size, a high level of agricultural productivity φ can now trigger industrialization by raising the endogenous level of population. This result is consistent with the early works of Nurkse (1953) and Murphy *et al.* (1989) and also supported by empirical evidence in recent studies by Olsson and Hibbs (2005) and Chu and Xu (2024), who find that favorable initial biogeographic conditions can contribute to economic development and industrialization.[9]

Furthermore, a high level of industrial productivity A and a low fixed cost δ of industrial production reduce the endogenous threshold by making industrial production more attractive and can also trigger industrialization. Finally, if the population size N_t reaches the industrial threshold N_I, then an industrial economy emerges and the

---

[9]Ang (2015) also finds that favorable initial biogeographic conditions can facilitate technology adoption as late as 1500 AD.

population growth rate rises toward a steady-state value, given by

$$\frac{\Delta N}{N} = \frac{\gamma}{\rho} A l - 1 \qquad (7.24)$$

as $N_t \to \infty$.

7.2.3 Dynamics of population growth

If the population manages to evolve from agriculture to industrial production, the dynamics of the population growth rate can be summarized as follows:

$$\frac{\Delta N_t}{N_t} = \frac{\gamma}{\rho}(x_t + f_t) - 1 = \begin{cases} \frac{\gamma}{\rho}\varphi l^\beta \left(\frac{Z}{N_t}\right)^{1-\beta} - 1 & \text{for } N_t < N_I \\ \frac{\gamma A}{\rho}\left(l - \frac{\delta}{N_t}\right) - 1 & \text{for } N_t > N_I \end{cases}.$$

$$(7.25)$$

Figure 7.2 plots the population growth rate $\Delta N_t/N_t$ for the following two scenarios: (a) the population does not experience industrialization and converges to an agricultural Malthusian trap, as discussed in Section 7.1.4; and (b) the population experiences the transition from

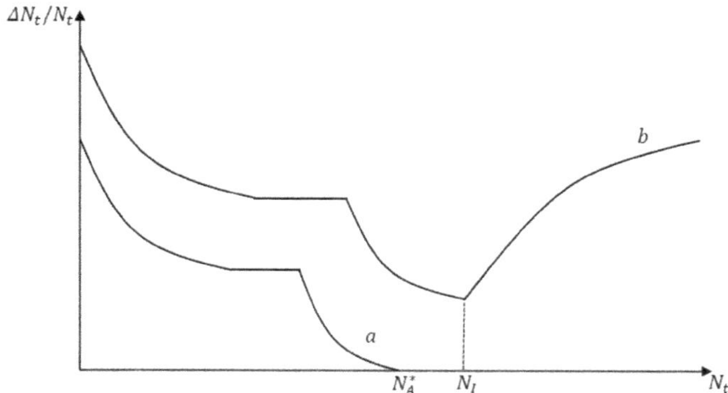

Figure 7.2. Dynamics of population growth.

agriculture to industrial production and achieves long-run growth, as discussed in Section 7.2.2.[10]

7.3   Summary and Discussion

In this chapter, we have extended the Malthusian growth model to capture the economic evolution of human society from agriculture to industrial production. We find that under endogenous population growth, the evolution of human society from an agricultural economy to an industrial economy is not inevitable. If the population size fails to reach the industrial threshold, then the human population remains in an agricultural society and stays in an agricultural Malthusian trap in the long run. Only if the population size reaches this threshold does industrialization occur and an industrial economy emerge.

Our model identifies several potential causes for the Industrial Revolution. One of these causes is a high level of industrial productivity (e.g., the invention of the steam engine). Another potential cause is a high level of agricultural productivity, and this theoretical result is also consistent with empirical evidence. A number of studies indeed find empirical support for high agricultural productivity contributing to a high level of economic development and a high degree of industrialization in modern times.[11]

Finally, an unrealistic prediction emerges from our theoretical model. The model predicts an immediate and complete transition from agriculture to industrial production, instead of a gradual industrial transition as observed in reality. The following chapter shows how a gradual industrial transition can be obtained in an extended Malthusian growth model with a market structure of monopolistic competition in the industrial economy.

---

[10]The first two portions of the two paths in Figure 7.2 originate from the transition from hunting-gathering to agriculture as in Figure 5.2.

[11]See, for example, Olsson and Hibbs (2005) and Chu and Xu (2024).

Chapter 8

Monopolistic Competition in the Industrial Era

In the previous chapter, we considered an industrial production function without specifying a market economy. This chapter presents a microeconomic foundation of the previous industrial production function, in which the fixed cost δ is now interpreted as a fixed operation cost incurred by firms with monopolistic power over their products.[1] As North and Thomas (1973, p. 156) write, "England [...] by 1700 [...] had developed an efficient set of property rights embedded in the common law [and...] begun to protect private property in knowledge with its patent law. The stage was now set for the industrial revolution." Specifically, one can think of the industrial production function in (7.5) as a reduced-form representation of a market structure of monopolistic competition. In this extended Malthusian growth model with a market structure of monopolistic competition, the transition from agricultural production to industrial production can become gradual, and this gradual industrial transition is more consistent with the Industrial Revolution.

The intuition for this gradual industrial transition is that the wage rate of industrial labor becomes lower than its marginal product due

---

[1]This chapter is based on Chu and Xu (2024). The mathematical model of monopolistic competition originates from Dixit and Stiglitz (1977).

to monopolistic markup pricing. As a result, agents may not allocate all their labor to industrial production, at least not immediately. Although the industrial transition becomes gradual, the rest of the implications remain largely the same. In other words, if and only if the population size reaches the industrial threshold, then an industrial economy emerges. As before, industrialization can be triggered by a high level of agricultural productivity, a low cost of fertility, a strong preference for fertility, a high level of industrial productivity, and a low fixed cost of operating industrial firms. Interestingly, during the gradual industrial transition, the economy may experience a rise or a decline in the population growth rate. Furthermore, the market structure of monopolistic competition in the industrial economy will also enable us to explore the emergence of innovation in the following chapter. As Jones (2019) writes, "imperfect competition provides the profits that incentivize entrepreneurs to innovate."

8.1   Monopolistic Market in the Industrial Economy

We replace the reduced-form production function for industrial output X_t in (7.5) with a market structure of monopolistic competition with a standard CES aggregator:

$$X_t = \left\{ \int_0^1 [X_t(j)]^\varepsilon \, dj \right\}^{1/\varepsilon}, \tag{8.1}$$

where $\varepsilon \in (0,1)$ determines the elasticity $1/(1-\varepsilon)$ of substitution between differentiated intermediate goods $X_t(j)$ indexed by $j \in [0,1]$. Profit maximization by competitive firms for producing X_t yields the conditional demand function for intermediate good j:

$$X_t(j) = \left[\frac{p_t}{p_t(j)} \right]^{1/(1-\varepsilon)} X_t \Leftrightarrow p_t(j) = p_t \left[\frac{X_t}{X_t(j)} \right]^{1-\varepsilon}, \tag{8.2}$$

where p_t and $p_t(j)$ are, respectively, the prices of X_t and $X_t(j)$ for $j \in [0,1]$.

Following Krugman (1979), operating an industrial firm requires a fixed cost $\delta > 0$ under which the production function of intermediate good j is given by

$$X_t(j) = A[l_{X,t}(j) - \delta], \tag{8.3}$$

where $l_{X,t}(j)$ is labor devoted to the production of intermediate good j. The profit function of the monopolistic firm that produces intermediate good j is

$$\pi_t(j) = p_t(j)X_t(j) - w_t l_{X,t}(j) = p_t X_t^{1-\varepsilon}[X_t(j)]^\varepsilon - w_t \left[\frac{X_t(j)}{A} + \delta\right], \tag{8.4}$$

where w_t is the wage rate of industrial labor. Profit maximization by the monopolistic firm yields markup pricing:

$$p_t(j) = \frac{1}{\varepsilon}\frac{w_t}{A} > \frac{w_t}{A}, \tag{8.5}$$

where $1/\varepsilon > 1$ is the markup ratio and w_t/A is the marginal cost of producing $X_t(j)$.

The amount of monopolistic profit for firm j is

$$\pi_t(j) = p_t(j)A[l_{X,t}(j) - \delta] - w_t l_{X,t}(j) = \frac{1-\varepsilon}{\varepsilon}w_t \left[l_{X,t}(j) - \frac{\delta}{1-\varepsilon}\right], \tag{8.6}$$

which is positive if and only if $l_{X,t}(j) > \delta/(1 - \varepsilon)$ for $j \in [0, 1]$. Substituting (8.5) into (8.2) yields a symmetric level of industrial output $X_t(j) = X_t$ in (8.1) and also a symmetric level of industrial labor $l_{X,t}(j) = l_{X,t}N_t$, where $l_{X,t}$ is each agent's labor devoted to industrial production. Therefore, we have

$$\pi_t(j) = \pi_t > 0 \Leftrightarrow l_{X,t}(j) = l_{X,t}N_t > \frac{\delta}{1 - \varepsilon}.$$

In other words, due to the fixed operation cost δ, the industrial market would not operate unless population N_t is sufficiently large. Substituting $l_{X,t}(j) = l_{X,t}N_t$ into (8.3) yields

$$X_t(j) = X_t = A(l_{X,t}N_t - \delta),$$

as in (7.5), which in turn implies that the per capita level of industrial output is given by

$$x_t = A\left(l_{X,t} - \frac{\delta}{N_t}\right),$$

as in (7.6).

8.1.1 Agriculture versus industrial production

To be consistent with our model in Chapter 7, agents may also produce food output f_t for consumption c_t and raising children ρn_t. As before, maximizing utility

$$u_t = (1 - \gamma)\ln c_t + \gamma \ln n_t$$

subject to $c_t = y_t - \rho n_t$ yields the population growth rate, given by

$$\frac{\Delta N_t}{N_t} = n_t - 1 = \frac{\gamma}{\rho}y_t - 1,$$

where the per capita level of total output is $y_t = f_t + x_t$.

The agents may purchase industrial output x_t (when available) and pay for it using their industrial wage income $w_t l_{X,t}$. Therefore, in the industrial era, each agent maximizes $y_t = f_t + x_t$ subject to farming production in (7.2), labor constraint $l_{F,t} + l_{X,t} = l$, and the following budget constraint:

$$p_t x_t = w_t l_{X,t} + \frac{1}{N_t}\int_0^1 \pi_t(j)dj, \tag{8.7}$$

where profits $\pi_t(j) \geq 0$ from all monopolistic firms $j \in [0,1]$ are redistributed to all N_t agents equally. The first-order condition is

$$\frac{\partial y_t}{\partial l_{F,t}} = \frac{\partial(f_t + x_t)}{\partial l_{F,t}} = \underbrace{\beta\varphi(l_{F,t})^{\beta-1}\left(\frac{Z}{N_t}\right)^{1-\beta}}_{\equiv MPL_F} - \frac{w_t}{p_t}, \tag{8.8}$$

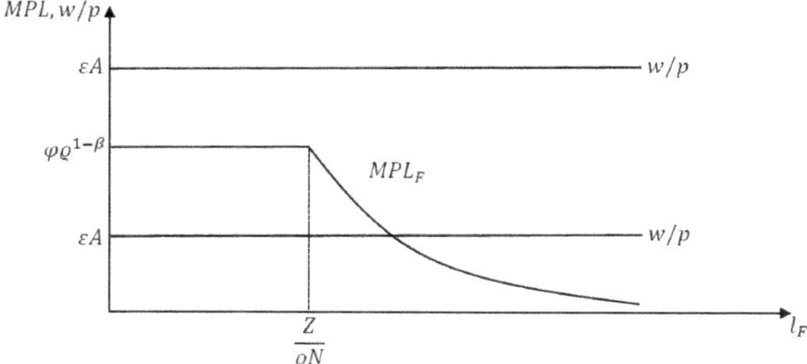

Figure 8.1. Labor market.

where $w_t/p_t = w_t/p_t(j) = \varepsilon A$ from imposing symmetry in (8.2) and using markup pricing in (8.5).

Figure 8.1 plots (8.8) and shows that there are two scenarios: (a) an interior solution (i.e., $\{l_{F,t}, l_{X,t}\} \in (0, l)$ under $\varphi \varrho^{1-\beta} > \varepsilon A$) which gives rise to a gradual transition from agriculture to industrial production, and (b) a corner solution (i.e., $l_{F,t} = 0$ and $l_{X,t} = l$ under $\varphi \varrho^{1-\beta} < \varepsilon A$) which gives rise to an immediate transition. Recall that we have only assumed $\varphi \varrho^{1-\beta} < A$ in Chapter 7 but $\varepsilon < 1$.

8.2 Gradual Transition to Industrial Production

If $\varphi \varrho^{1-\beta} > \varepsilon A$, then the equilibrium level of agricultural labor $l_{F,t}$ from (8.8) is

$$l_{F,t} = \left(\frac{\beta\varphi}{\varepsilon A}\right)^{1/(1-\beta)} \frac{Z}{N_t}, \tag{8.9}$$

which implies that the equilibrium level of industrial labor is

$$l_{X,t} = l - l_{F,t} = l - \left(\frac{\beta\varphi}{\varepsilon A}\right)^{1/(1-\beta)} \frac{Z}{N_t}. \tag{8.10}$$

An industrial market would only emerge if N_t is sufficiently large to cover the fixed cost δ such that $l_{X,t} N_t \geq \delta/(1-\varepsilon)$, which is required for nonnegative profit $\pi_t(j) \geq 0$. Then, (8.10) yields

$$N_t \geq \frac{1}{l}\left[\left(\frac{\beta\varphi}{\varepsilon A}\right)^{1/(1-\beta)} Z + \frac{\delta}{1-\varepsilon}\right] \equiv N_I(\underset{+}{\varphi}, \underset{+}{Z}, \underset{+}{\delta}, \underset{-}{A}, \underset{-}{l}), \qquad (8.11)$$

which is now given by a closed-form solution and has the same comparative statics as (7.9).

Before the emergence of industrial production, the population growth rate $\Delta N_t/N_t$ and the steady-state population level N_A^* in the agricultural era are given by (7.19),

$$\frac{\Delta N_t}{N_t} = \frac{\gamma}{\rho}\varphi l^\beta \left(\frac{Z}{N_t}\right)^{1-\beta} - 1,$$

and (7.20),

$$N_A^* = \left(\frac{\gamma}{\rho}\varphi l^\beta\right)^{1/(1-\beta)} Z,$$

as in Chapter 7. If N_t reaches N_A^* before reaching N_I (i.e., $N_A^* < N_I$), then the population remains as an agricultural society indefinitely; otherwise, an industrial transition occurs. From (7.20) and (8.11), the inequality $N_A^* > N_I$ is equivalent to

$$\left(\frac{\gamma l}{\rho}\right)^{1/(1-\beta)} > \left(\frac{\beta}{\varepsilon A}\right)^{1/(1-\beta)} + \frac{\delta}{(1-\varepsilon)\varphi^{1/(1-\beta)}Z}, \qquad (8.12)$$

which shows that the transition from an agricultural economy to an industrial economy occurs under the following conditions: a low fertility cost ρ, a strong fertility preference γ, a high level of agricultural productivity φ, a high level of labor supply l, a large amount of land Z, a high level of industrial productivity A, and a low fixed cost δ of operating industrial firms. These conditions are the same as in Chapter 7, except that the transition in this case is gradual (i.e., $l_{F,t} > 0$ and $l_{X,t} < l$ until $N_t \to \infty$).

Under the interior solution, the level of total output per capita in the industrial era is given by

$$y_t = f_t + x_t = \varphi(l_{F,t})^\beta \left(\frac{Z}{N_t}\right)^{1-\beta} + A\left(l - l_{F,t} - \frac{\delta}{N_t}\right), \qquad (8.13)$$

which is decreasing in $l_{F,t}$ because (8.8) implies that $\beta\varphi(l_{F,t})^{\beta-1}(Z/N_t)^{1-\beta} = w_t/p_t = \varepsilon A < A$. Then, (8.9) shows that $l_{F,t}$ is decreasing in N_t. Substituting (8.9) and (8.13) into

$$\frac{\Delta N_t}{N_t} = \frac{\gamma}{\rho}y_t - 1 = \frac{\gamma}{\rho}(x_t + f_t) - 1 \qquad (8.14)$$

yields the population growth rate, which, as before, converges toward the same steady state $\Delta N/N = \frac{\gamma}{\rho}Al - 1$ as $N_t \to \infty$. Interestingly, the population growth rate may rise toward $\Delta N/N = \frac{\gamma}{\rho}Al - 1$ as before or fall toward this steady state. Substituting (8.9) and (8.13) into (8.14) yields

$$\frac{\Delta N_t}{N_t} = \frac{\gamma}{\rho}\left(Al + \frac{\Phi}{N_t}\right) - 1, \qquad (8.15)$$

where the composite parameter Φ is defined as

$$\Phi \equiv A\left[\left(\frac{\varepsilon}{\beta} - 1\right)\left(\frac{\beta\varphi}{\varepsilon A}\right)^{1/(1-\beta)} Z - \delta\right],$$

which can be positive or negative. If $\Phi < 0$, then the population growth rate is rising in the industrial era as before; see Figure 8.2.

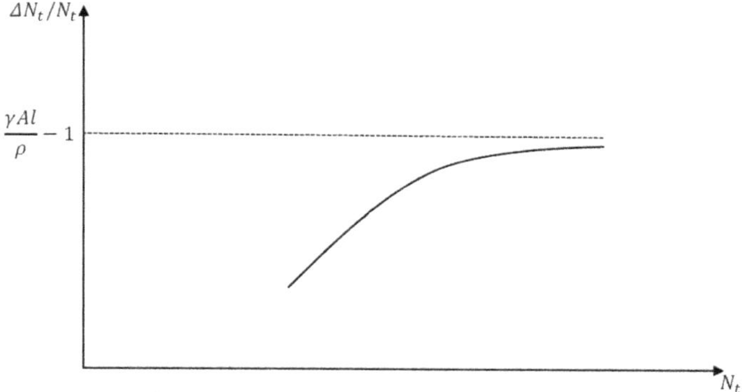

Figure 8.2.   Rising population growth in the industrial era.

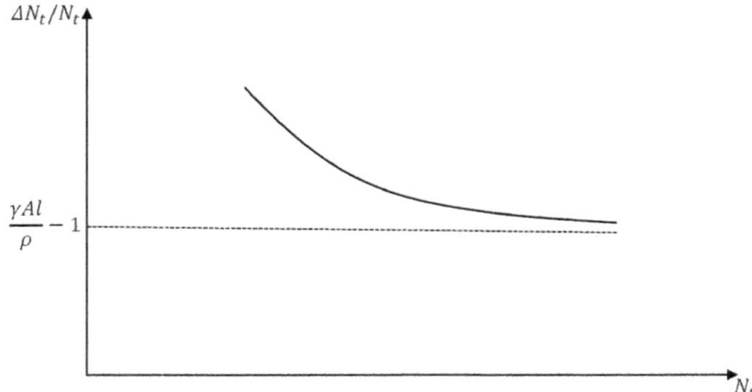

Figure 8.3.   Declining population growth in the industrial era.

If $\Phi > 0$, then the population growth rate is falling in the industrial era; see Figure 8.3.

8.3   Immediate Transition to Industrial Production

If $\varphi\varrho^{1-\beta} < \varepsilon A$, then the level of industrial labor $l_{X,t}$ increases sharply from 0 to l when N_t crosses the threshold $N_I \equiv \delta/[(1-\varepsilon)l]$. In this case, the inequality $N_A^* > N_I$ is equivalent to

$$(1-\varepsilon)\left(\frac{\gamma}{\rho}\varphi l\right)^{1/(1-\beta)}\frac{Z}{\delta} > 1, \tag{8.16}$$

which uses (7.20) and has the same comparative statics for $\{\rho, \gamma, \varphi, l, Z, \delta\}$, as in Chapter 7. In other words, the transition from an agricultural economy to an industrial economy occurs under the following conditions: a low fertility cost ρ, a strong fertility preference γ, a high level of agricultural productivity φ, a high level of labor supply l, a large amount of land Z, and a low fixed cost δ of operating industrial firms. These conditions are also the same as in Chapter 7. The only exception is industrial productivity A; however, a larger A can still trigger industrialization by making the corner solution more likely to apply via a reduction in the threshold N_I from (8.11) to $N_I \equiv \delta/[(1-\varepsilon)l]$.

It is useful to note that although the industrial transition is immediate in this case, $N_I \equiv \delta/[(1 - \varepsilon)l]$ is not the same as N_I in (7.8) and (7.9). Also, there exists a value of $\varepsilon \in (0, 1)$ above which $\delta/[(1 - \varepsilon)l]$ is greater than N_I in (7.8) and (7.9). In this case, industrialization occurs later because the markup ratio $1/\varepsilon$ is too small to cover the fixed cost δ. Finally, under the corner solution, the level of industrial output per capita $y_t = x_t$ is the same as (7.12),

$$y_t = x_t = A\left(l - \frac{\delta}{N_t}\right),$$

and the population growth rate in the industrial era is the same as (7.21),

$$\frac{\Delta N_t}{N_t} = \frac{\gamma A}{\rho}\left(l - \frac{\delta}{N_t}\right) - 1.$$

In this case, the population growth rate rises toward the same steady state $\Delta N/N = \frac{\gamma}{\rho}Al - 1$ as in Figure 8.2.

8.4　Summary and Discussion

In this chapter, we have provided a microeconomic foundation of our reduced-form industrial production function in Chapter 7. Specifically, we interpreted the fixed cost δ as a fixed operation cost incurred by firms with monopolistic power over their products in a monopolistic market in the industrial economy. Because monopolistic markup pricing reduces the wage rate of industrial labor below its marginal product, agents may not immediately allocate all their labor to industrial production. In this case, the transition from agriculture to industrial production becomes gradual, unlike the immediate industrial transition in Chapter 7, which is not as realistic.

Although the industrial transition becomes gradual, the rest of the previous implications remain largely unchanged, confirming the robustness of our results. In other words, the population size needs to reach an industrial threshold in order for industrialization to occur and for an industrial economy to emerge. As before, industrialization can be triggered by a high level of agricultural productivity, a low cost of fertility, a strong preference for fertility, a high level of industrial productivity, and a low fixed cost of industrial operation.

Finally, the market structure of monopolistic competition in the industrial economy provides the necessary environment for us to consider the emergence of market-driven innovation and technological progress in the post-industrial economy. In the following chapter, we explore the importance of education and human capital accumulation on the emergence of innovation-driven growth in the post-industrial era.

Part IV

Post-Industrial Era

Chapter 9

Education and Innovation-Driven Growth

> In the earliest phase of the Industrial Revolution, literacy and numeracy played a limited role in the production process. [...] During the subsequent phases of the Industrial Revolution, the demand for skilled labour in the growing industrial sector markedly increased. From here on, and for the first time in history, human capital formation—factors that influence workers productivity, such as education, training, skills and health—was designed and undertaken with the primary purpose of satisfying the increasing requirements of industrialisation. (Galor 2022, p. 67)

The previous chapter considers the emergence of a market structure of monopolistic competition in the early phase of the industrial era, in which the increasing returns to scale in industrial production enables the economy to escape from the agricultural Malthusian trap. During the later phases of the industrial era, education and innovation become important because "enhanced human capital facilitated further technological advancement."[1] Therefore, this chapter explores how education and the accumulation of human capital affect the emergence of innovation and technological progress.[2]

---

[1]See Galor (2022, p. 71).

[2]The model in this chapter is an extended version of the one presented by Chu *et al.* (2022b) with the addition of endogenous fertility. For studies on the

Specifically, we develop an innovation-driven growth model with endogenous fertility and two stages of economic development. In the first stage of development, economic growth is driven by only human capital accumulation. In the second stage, economic growth is driven by both innovation and human capital accumulation. Within this growth-theoretic framework, we find that the level of human capital in the population needs to accumulate to a sufficient level before innovation emerges. If the level of human capital does not reach this threshold in the long run, then the economy eventually becomes stagnant and does not experience the transition to innovation and long-run economic growth. In this case, the size of the population grows at a constant rate, but industrial output per capita converges to a steady-state level without growth, as in the previous chapter. If the level of human capital rises above the innovation threshold, then innovation emerges to generate long-run growth in the level of output per capita via the continuous development of new products (such as automobiles, computers, and smartphones), which captures the essence of a modern economy.

Interestingly, a strong fertility preference makes the no-growth trap more likely to occur by crowding out parental investment in education. The effects of fertility preference differ across industrialization in the previous chapter and technological progress in this chapter because the former requires a large market size, whereas the latter requires a high level of human capital. Furthermore, high R&D productivity and high education productivity make the no-growth trap less likely to occur. Finally, an education preference that is either too weak or too strong makes the no-growth trap more likely to occur. The intuition is that a weak education preference

---

endogenous transition from pre-industrial stagnation to innovation-driven growth, see also Peretto (1999, 2015), Funke and Strulik (2000), Jones (2001), Kalemli-Ozcan (2002), Iacopetta (2010), Chu *et al.* (2020a, 2020b, 2022a, 2022c, 2023), Iacopetta and Peretto (2021), and Chu and Peretto (2023).

gives rise to a low level of human capital, whereas a strong education preference causes overinvestment in human capital that crowds out resources for innovation. This last result captures a potential explanation for the Needham puzzle on why modern innovation did not happen in Imperial China, proposed by Lin (1995, p. 284) that "China's failure to make the transition from premodern science to modern science probably had something to do with [...] the incentive structure of the system [that] diverted the intelligentsia away from scientific endeavors."

9.1 An Innovation-Driven Growth Model with Endogenous Fertility and Education

The innovation-driven growth model is based on the seminal work of Romer (1990).[3] We consider endogenous fertility as in previous chapters and modify the Romer model by incorporating a similar structure of overlapping generations as before and also human capital accumulation.[4] Each agent now lives for three periods as life expectancy rises after industrialization. In youth, the agent accumulates human capital. In working age, the agent allocates time between work, fertility, and education of the next generation. In old age, the agent consumes the saving.[5] For simplicity, we assume that

---

[3]For other early studies on innovation-driven growth, see also Aghion and Howitt (1992), Grossman and Helpman (1991), and Segerstrom *et al.* (1990).

[4]For early studies that introduce human capital accumulation to the Romer model, see Eicher (1996) and Zeng (1997). For early studies on endogenous fertility and innovation, see Jones (2001, 2003), Connolly and Peretto (2003), and Growiec (2006). Becker *et al.* (1990) provide the first study that combines endogenous fertility and human capital accumulation in an endogenous growth model, whereas Chu *et al.* (2013) develop a Schumpeterian growth model with both endogenous fertility and human capital accumulation.

[5]This assumption is for simplicity. Our results are robust to agents having consumption in both their working age and old age.

the transition from agriculture to an industrial economy is already completed, so that all output Y_t comes from industrial production.

9.1.1   Endogenous fertility and education

The utility of an adult agent who works at time t is given by

$$u_t = (1 - \gamma) \ln c_{t+1} + \gamma \ln n_t + \kappa \ln h_{t+1}, \tag{9.1}$$

where c_{t+1} is the agent's consumption in old age, n_t is the number of children, and $\gamma \in (0, 1)$ is the degree of fertility preference as before. h_{t+1} denotes the level of human capital that the agent passes onto each child, and the new parameter $\kappa \geq 0$ is the degree of education preference.

The agent allocates e_t units of time to the children's education. The accumulation equation of human capital is given by

$$h_{t+1} = \xi e_t + (1 - d)h_t, \tag{9.2}$$

where $d \in (0, 1)$ is the human capital depreciation rate. The parameter $\xi > 0$ determines productivity in the education process.[6] An agent allocates $1 - e_t - \rho n_t$ units of time to work and earns $(1 - e_t - \rho n_t)w_t h_t$ as real wage income, where w_t is the wage rate and the parameter $\rho \in (0, 1)$ determines the time cost of fertility.[7] The agent saves all of the wage income at time t and then consumes the return at time $t + 1$:

$$c_{t+1} = (1 + r_{t+1})(1 - e_t - \rho n_t)w_t h_t, \tag{9.3}$$

where r_{t+1} is the real interest rate.

---

[6]This parameter could be influenced by the schooling system, which we do not model here.

[7]In this chapter, we consider fertility cost in terms of parents' time to ensure a steady-state (instead of a rising) population growth rate when there is growth in output per capita. Implicitly, we are assuming that parents' time becomes the most important input in childrearing in modern society.

Substituting (9.2) and (9.3) into (9.1), the agent maximizes

$$\max_{e_t, n_t} u_t = (1 - \gamma)\ln[(1 + r_{t+1})(1 - e_t - \rho n_t)w_t h_t]$$

$$+ \gamma \ln n_t + \kappa \ln[\xi e_t + (1 - d)h_t],$$

taking $\{r_{t+1}, w_t, h_t\}$ as given. The utility-maximizing level of fertility n_t is

$$n_t = \frac{\gamma}{\rho(1 + \kappa)}\left[1 + (1 - d)\frac{h_t}{\xi}\right], \tag{9.4}$$

which is decreasing in education preference κ and education productivity ξ but increasing in fertility preference γ and human capital h_t. The utility-maximizing level of education e_t is[8]

$$e_t = \frac{\kappa}{1 + \kappa}\left[1 - (1 - d)\frac{h_t}{\xi\kappa}\right], \tag{9.5}$$

which is increasing in education preference κ and education productivity ξ but decreasing in human capital h_t. In summary, for a given h_t, an increase in education preference κ or education productivity ξ gives rise to a higher level of education e_t but a smaller number n_t of children, reflecting the quality–quantity trade-off.

9.1.2 Dynamics of human capital and population

Substituting (9.5) into (9.2) yields the autonomous and stable dynamics of human capital as

$$h_{t+1} = \frac{\kappa}{1 + \kappa}[\xi + (1 - d)h_t], \tag{9.6}$$

where the next generation's human capital h_{t+1} is increasing in education preference κ, education productivity ξ, and the current

---

[8]We impose $h_0 < \xi\kappa$ to ensure $e_t \geq 0$ for all t.

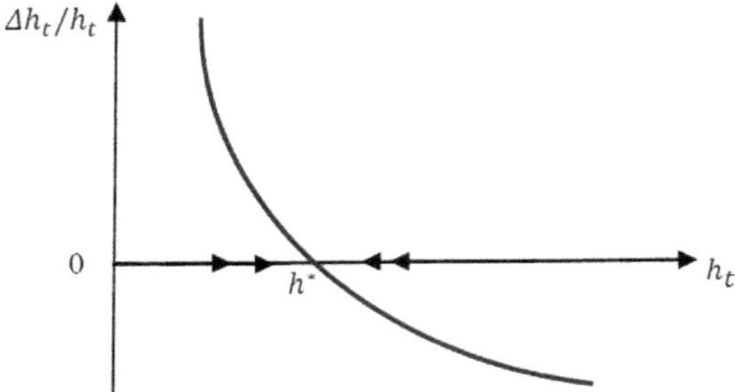

Figure 9.1.　Dynamics of human capital.

generation's human capital h_t. From (9.6), the growth rate of human capital can be expressed as

$$\frac{\Delta h_t}{h_t} \equiv \frac{h_{t+1} - h_t}{h_t} = \frac{1}{1+\kappa}\left[\frac{\xi\kappa}{h_t} - (1 + \kappa d)\right].$$

Figure 9.1 shows that human capital h_t converges to its steady-state level h^*.

The total amount of human capital of the working generation at time t is

$$H_t = h_t N_t,$$

where N_t is the working-age population size. The law of motion for N_t is

$$N_{t+1} = n_t N_t = \frac{\gamma}{\rho(1+\kappa)}\left[1 + (1-d)\frac{h_t}{\xi}\right] N_t,$$

and the growth rate of N_t is

$$\frac{\Delta N_t}{N_t} = \frac{\gamma}{\rho(1+\kappa)}\left[1 + (1-d)\frac{h_t}{\xi}\right] - 1, \tag{9.7}$$

which will be referred to as the population growth rate. As human capital h_t converges to its steady state h^*, population growth also converges to the steady-state growth rate.

9.1.3 Industrial output

Competitive firms produce final output Y_t (chosen as the numeraire) using the following production function[9]:

$$Y_t = (H_{Y,t})^{1-\varepsilon} \int_0^{A_t} [X_t(j)]^\varepsilon \, dj, \tag{9.8}$$

where the parameter $\varepsilon \in (0,1)$ determines both the elasticity $1/(1-\varepsilon)$ of substitution between intermediate goods $X_t(j)$ as before and also labor intensity $1-\varepsilon$ in the production process, whereas $H_{Y,t}$ denotes human-capital-embodied production labor. $X_t(j)$ denotes a continuum of differentiated intermediate goods indexed by $j \in [0, A_t]$, where the mass of differentiated intermediate goods A_t determines industrial productivity and may grow endogenously. Firms maximize profit, and the conditional demand functions for $H_{Y,t}$ and $X_t(j)$ are given by

$$w_t = (1-\varepsilon)\frac{Y_t}{H_{Y,t}}, \tag{9.9}$$

$$p_t(j) = \varepsilon \left[\frac{H_{Y,t}}{X_t(j)}\right]^{1-\varepsilon}, \tag{9.10}$$

where $p_t(j)$ is the price of $X_t(j)$.

9.1.4 Intermediate goods

Each intermediate good j is produced by a monopolistic firm, which uses a one-to-one linear production function that transforms $X_t(j)$

---

[9]We consider a different aggregator from Chapter 8 for consistency with Romer (1990).

units of final good into $X_t(j)$ units of intermediate good $j \in [0, A_t]$.[10]
The profit function is

$$\pi_t(j) = p_t(j)X_t(j) - X_t(j), \tag{9.11}$$

where the marginal cost of production is constant and equal to one
(recall that final good is the numeraire). The monopolistic firm maximizes (9.11) subject to (9.10) to derive the profit-maximizing price
as

$$p_t(j) = \frac{1}{\varepsilon} > 1, \tag{9.12}$$

where $1/\varepsilon$ is the markup ratio as before and the marginal cost of
production is one. One can show that $X_t(j) = X_t$ for all $j \in [0, A_t]$ by
substituting (9.12) into (9.10). Then, we substitute (9.10) and (9.12)
into (9.11) to derive the amount of profit for the monopolistic firm
in each industry j as

$$\pi_t(j) = \pi_t = \frac{1-\varepsilon}{\varepsilon}X_t = (1-\varepsilon)\varepsilon^{(1+\varepsilon)/(1-\varepsilon)}H_{Y,t} > 0. \tag{9.13}$$

9.1.5   Innovation

We denote v_t as the value of a newly invented intermediate good at
the end of time t. The value v_t is determined by the present value of
profits from time $t + 1$ onward:

$$v_t = \sum_{\tau=t+1}^{\infty}\left[\pi_\tau \left/ \prod_{\iota=t+1}^{\tau}(1+r_\iota)\right.\right]. \tag{9.14}$$

Competitive R&D entrepreneurs invent new products by employing
$H_{R,t}$ units of human-capital-embodied labor. We specify the following

---

[10]Instead of a fixed operation cost, we consider an R&D cost in the following section, which also generates an increasing returns to scale because an entrepreneur
needs to incur the cost of acquiring an invention before producing the intermediate good; see Romer (1990) for a detailed discussion.

innovation process:

$$\Delta A_t = \frac{\vartheta A_t H_{R,t}}{N_t},\tag{9.15}$$

where $\Delta A_t \equiv A_{t+1} - A_t$ is the number of newly invented intermediate goods at the end of time t. The parameter $\vartheta > 0$ determines R&D productivity $\vartheta A_t/N_t$, where A_t captures intertemporal knowledge spillovers, as given by Romer (1990), and $1/N_t$ captures a dilution effect that removes the scale effect and ensures a balanced growth path in the presence of population growth.[11] If the following free-entry condition holds:

$$\Delta A_t v_t = w_t H_{R,t} \Leftrightarrow \frac{\vartheta A_t v_t}{N_t} = w_t,\tag{9.16}$$

then R&D $H_{R,t}$ would be positive at time t. If $\vartheta A_t v_t/N_t < w_t$, then R&D does not take place at time t (i.e., $H_{R,t} = 0$).

9.1.6 Aggregation

The key condition for solving this overlapping-generation version of the Romer model is that the savings $(1 - e_t - \rho n_t)w_t h_t$ of all agents N_t at time t is equal to the value of all assets $A_{t+1}v_t$ at the end of time t such that

$$(1 - e_t - \rho n_t)w_t h_t N_t = A_{t+1}v_t.\tag{9.17}$$

Then, imposing symmetry on (9.8) yields $Y_t = H_{Y,t}^{1-\varepsilon}A_t X_t^{\varepsilon}$. We substitute (9.10) and (9.12) into this equation to derive the aggregate production function as

$$Y_t = \varepsilon^{2\varepsilon/(1-\varepsilon)}A_t H_{Y,t}.\tag{9.18}$$

Using $A_t X_t = \varepsilon^2 Y_t$, we obtain the following resource constraint on the final good:

$$C_t = Y_t - A_t X_t = (1 - \varepsilon^2)Y_t,\tag{9.19}$$

---

[11]See Jones (1999) and Laincz and Peretto (2006) for a discussion of the scale effect.

where $C_t = c_t N_{t-1}$ denotes total consumption at time t by the old generation. Finally, the resource constraint on human-capital-embodied labor of the working generation at time t is

$$(1 - e_t - \rho n_t) h_t N_t = H_{Y,t} + H_{R,t}. \tag{9.20}$$

9.2 Stages of Economic Development

Our model features two stages of development in the industrial era. The first stage features only human capital accumulation. The second stage features both human capital accumulation and innovation. The emergence of innovation is endogenous, and the transition from the first stage to the second stage does not necessarily occur.

9.2.1 Stage 1: Human capital accumulation only

At time 0, the initial level of human capital for each agent is h_0. Suppose the following inequality holds:

$$\frac{1}{\vartheta} > (1 - e_0 - \rho n_0) h_0 = \frac{1 - \gamma}{1 + \kappa} \left[1 + (1 - d) \frac{h_0}{\xi} \right] h_0, \tag{9.21}$$

where the equality uses (9.4) and (9.5). Then, substituting $1/\vartheta > (1 - e_0 - \rho n_0) h_0$ into (9.17) yields $w_t > \vartheta A_{t+1} v_t / N_t \geq \vartheta A_t v_t / N_t$, which implies that $H_{R,0} = 0$ from (9.16). In this case, all human-capital-embodied labor is devoted to the production of industrial output:

$$H_{Y,0} = (1 - e_0 - \rho n_0) h_0 N_0 = \frac{1 - \gamma}{1 + \kappa} \left[1 + (1 - d) \frac{h_0}{\xi} \right] h_0 N_0. \tag{9.22}$$

In this stage of development, the economy features only human capital accumulation. Human capital h_t gradually accumulates according to the autonomous and stable dynamics in (9.6). However, so long as the following inequality holds at time t:

$$\frac{1}{\vartheta} > (1 - e_t - \rho n_t)h_t = \frac{1 - \gamma}{1 + \kappa}\left[1 + (1 - d)\frac{h_t}{\xi}\right]h_t, \qquad (9.23)$$

we continue to have $H_{R,t} = 0$ and

$$H_{Y,t} = (1 - e_t - \rho n_t)h_t N_t = \frac{1 - \gamma}{1 + \kappa}\left[1 + (1 - d)\frac{h_t}{\xi}\right]h_t N_t, \qquad (9.24)$$

where the growth rate of N_t is determined by (9.7). Substituting (9.24) into (9.18) yields the per capita level of output as

$$y_t \equiv \frac{Y_t}{N_t} = \varepsilon^{2\varepsilon/(1-\varepsilon)} A_0 \frac{H_{Y,t}}{N_t} = \varepsilon^{2\varepsilon/(1-\varepsilon)} A_0 \frac{1 - \gamma}{1 + \kappa}\left[1 + (1 - d)\frac{h_t}{\xi}\right]h_t, \qquad (9.25)$$

where the mass of differentiated intermediate goods A_0 remains at the initial level and the per capita level of output increases only as human capital h_t accumulates. As human capital h_t reaches its steady state h^* (to be derived in the following), the per capita level of output y_t also reaches its steady state y^*, unless technological progress emerges (i.e., growth in A_t).

9.2.2 Does innovation emerge?

Equation (9.6) shows that the level of human capital h_t converges to the following steady-state value:

$$h^* = \frac{\xi \kappa}{1 + \kappa d}, \qquad (9.26)$$

which is increasing in education preference κ and education productivity ξ. Substituting (9.26) into (9.4) and (9.5) yields the steady-state levels of education and fertility, given by

$$e^* = \frac{\kappa d}{1 + \kappa d}, \qquad (9.27)$$

$$n^* = \frac{\gamma}{\rho(1 + \kappa d)}, \qquad (9.28)$$

respectively, where the endogenous fertility rate n^* is increasing in fertility preference γ but decreasing in fertility cost ρ, as before.

The population features positive population growth in the long run so long as $\gamma > \rho(1 + \kappa d)$, which ensures

$$\frac{\Delta N}{N} = n^* - 1 = \frac{\gamma}{\rho(1 + \kappa d)} - 1 > 0.$$

Does innovation emerge? If and only if the following inequality holds:

$$\frac{1}{\vartheta} < \left(1 - e^* - \rho n^*\right) h^* = \frac{(1 - \gamma)\xi\kappa}{(1 + \kappa d)^2}, \tag{9.29}$$

then human capital accumulation eventually triggers the emergence of innovation, under which the R&D condition in (9.16) holds and R&D $H_{R,t}$ becomes positive before human capital h_t reaches its steady-state value h^* in (9.26). Equation (9.29) holds under high R&D productivity ϑ, high education productivity ξ, and weak fertility preference γ. This negative effect of fertility preference γ on the emergence of innovation arises because technological progress requires human capital, but fertility crowds out parental investment in education. Furthermore, (9.29) holds under an intermediate degree of education preference κ because a weak education preference gives rise to a low level of human capital whereas a strong education preference causes overinvestment in human capital that crowds out resources for innovation.

9.2.3 Stage 2: Innovation and human capital accumulation

Suppose (9.29) holds. Then, to derive the equilibrium growth rate in the presence of innovation, we first substitute (9.18) into (9.9) to derive the equilibrium wage rate as

$$w_t = (1 - \varepsilon)\varepsilon^{2\varepsilon/(1-\varepsilon)} A_t. \tag{9.30}$$

Then, substituting (9.30) into (9.16) yields the equilibrium invention value as

$$v_t = \frac{(1 - \varepsilon)\varepsilon^{2\varepsilon/(1-\varepsilon)}}{\vartheta} N_t. \tag{9.31}$$

Because the value of assets at the end of time t is equal to the amount of savings at time t given by wage income, we have

$$A_{t+1}v_t = w_t(1 - e_t - \rho n_t)h_t N_t = w_t(H_{Y,t} + H_{R,t}), \tag{9.32}$$

where the second equality uses (9.20). Substituting (9.30) and (9.31) into (9.32) yields

$$A_{t+1} = \frac{\vartheta A_t}{N_t}(H_{Y,t} + H_{R,t}). \tag{9.33}$$

Combining (9.15) and (9.33) yields the equilibrium level of $H_{Y,t}$ as

$$\frac{H_{Y,t}}{N_t} = \frac{1}{\vartheta} \tag{9.34}$$

for all t. Substituting (9.4), (9.5), and (9.34) into (9.20) yields the equilibrium level of $H_{R,t} > 0$ as

$$\frac{H_{R,t}}{N_t} = (1 - e_t - \rho n_t)h_t - \frac{H_{Y,t}}{N_t} = \frac{1 - \gamma}{1 + \kappa}\left[1 + (1 - d)\frac{h_t}{\xi}\right]h_t - \frac{1}{\vartheta}. \tag{9.35}$$

We can now substitute (9.35) into (9.15) to derive the equilibrium growth rate of technology A_t as

$$g_t \equiv \frac{\Delta A_t}{A_t} = \frac{\vartheta H_{R,t}}{N_t} = \vartheta\frac{1 - \gamma}{1 + \kappa}\left[1 + (1 - d)\frac{h_t}{\xi}\right]h_t - 1, \tag{9.36}$$

which rises as human capital h_t accumulates. It is useful to note that g_t is also the equilibrium growth rate of industrial output per capita in stage 2 because

$$y_t = \frac{\varepsilon^{2\varepsilon/(1-\varepsilon)}}{\vartheta}A_t \Rightarrow \frac{\Delta y_t}{y_t} = \frac{\Delta A_t}{A_t}, \tag{9.37}$$

which uses (9.34). Finally, substituting (9.26) into (9.36) yields the steady-state equilibrium growth rate of A_t and y_t as

$$g^* = \frac{\vartheta(1 - \gamma)\xi\kappa}{(1 + \kappa d)^2} - 1, \tag{9.38}$$

which is increasing in R&D productivity ϑ and education productivity ξ but decreasing in fertility preference γ. The positive effects of

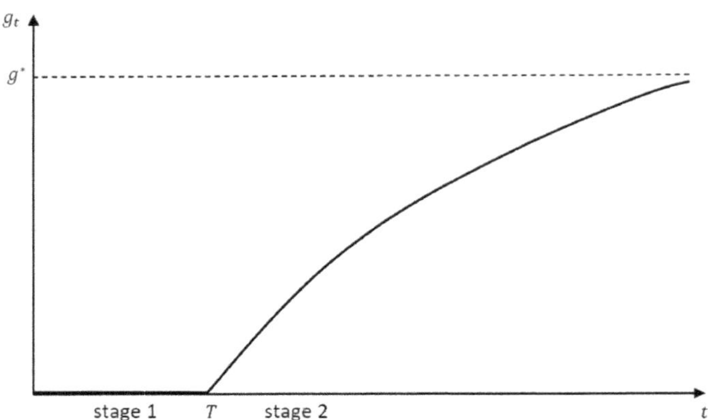

Figure 9.2. Dynamics of technology growth.

R&D productivity ϑ and education productivity ξ are quite intuitive, whereas the negative effect of fertility preference is due to its crowding out of parental investment in education. Furthermore, g^* is an inverted-U function of education preference κ due to the possibility of overinvestment in education.[12] Figure 9.2 plots the dynamics of the equilibrium growth rate of technology A_t and presents the case in which the transition from stage 1 to stage 2 occurs at time T.

9.3 Innovation under Negative Population Growth

In the above analysis, we assume $n^* = \gamma/[\rho(1 + \kappa d)] > 1$ in (9.28), which in turn implies a positive population growth rate $\Delta N/N = n^* - 1 > 0$, given that the world population has grown from roughly 1 billion in 1800 to 7.95 billion in 2022, according to the World Bank. The United Nations Population Division forecasts that the world population will reach 11 billion sometime in this century. However,

---

[12]This result originates from Chu *et al.* (2016), but their model does not feature endogenous fertility.

it is also possible that population growth will slow down and become negative at some point.[13]

Our growth-theoretic framework can easily generate a negative population growth rate. For example, a decrease in the degree of fertility preference γ such that $n^* = \gamma/[\rho(1+\kappa d)]$ falls below one gives rise to negative population growth. In this case, the world population will shrink and converge toward an empty planet (i.e., $N_t \to 0$), as discussed in Jones (2022). However, the long-run growth rate g^* of technology and output per capita in (9.38) actually rises when the degree of fertility preference γ goes down. This result stands in stark contrast to that reported by Jones (2022), whose model predicts a technology growth rate falling toward zero as the population size declines. This drastic difference arises because the growth rate g_t of technology depends on the average level of human capital in our model, rather than the total population size as in Jones (2022). Our result of a positive technology growth rate together with a negative population growth rate in the long run can also be obtained in the Schumpeterian growth model with an endogenous market structure by Peretto (2021), who also shows that negative population growth is fully compatible with positive economic growth.

9.4 Summary and Discussion

In this chapter, we have explored how the accumulation of human capital is necessary for the emergence of innovation and technological progress. We find that the level of human capital needs to accumulate to a sufficient level in order to trigger the transition from human capital accumulation to innovation-driven growth. It is possible that the level of human capital never reaches this threshold even in the long run. In this case, the economy exhibits a steady-state level of industrial output per capita and does not experience

---

[13]See, for example, Bricker and Ibbitson (2019).

technological progress. Interestingly, a strong fertility preference makes this pessimistic situation more likely to occur, whereas high R&D productivity and high education productivity make the no-growth trap less likely to occur. Furthermore, an education preference that is either too weak or too strong makes the no-growth trap more likely to occur. This last result captures a potential explanation proposed by Lin (1995) for the Needham puzzle that Imperial China did not make the transition to modern science because the system diverted too much resources and talent away from scientific research to education and examination.

If the level of human capital rises above the critical threshold, then innovation emerges to generate technological progress and long-run economic growth via the development of new products. This innovation process captures the essence of a modern economy. In this case, the long-run equilibrium growth rate of both technology and output per capita is positive and increasing in R&D productivity and education productivity but decreasing in fertility preference. A strong fertility preference has a negative effect on innovation because it crowds out parental investment in education. Interestingly, an education preference that is either too weak or too strong also stifles innovation. In the following chapter, we explore how the evolutionary process continues to exert its influence on the modern economy and surprisingly works against innovation and technological progress in the post-industrial era.

Chapter 10

Evolution of Innovation-Driven Growth

In the previous chapter, we consider an environment with homogeneous agents in each generation. In this chapter, we allow for heterogeneity across families to explore how the evolutionary process continues to affect innovation and technological progress in modern times. People have different levels of ability, so heterogeneity in education ability matters for human capital formation and gives rise to endogenous heterogeneity in fertility. How would the resulting evolutionary process influence technological progress and economic growth? To explore this question, we extend the Romer model with endogenous fertility in the previous chapter to allow for heterogeneous agents who differ in the ability to educate their children.[1]

Our model features two types of families, which differ in their ability to accumulate human capital. In this case, families that are more able to provide high-quality learning focus on child quality and have fewer children than less able families.[2] This quality–quantity trade-off

---

[1]The model in this chapter is a simplified version of the one given by Chu *et al.* (2024a). We focus on only two types of families here, whereas Chu *et al.* (2024a) consider an arbitrary number of family types.

[2]This negative relationship between child quantity and quality is consistent with the empirical evidence reported by Fernihough (2017) and Klemp and Weisdorf (2019).

in turn magnifies the share of less able families in the economy, at least temporarily. In an early stage of development, families that have a lower education ability accumulate less human capital but choose to have more children and enjoy an evolutionary advantage. In a later stage of development, families with a higher education ability choose to increase their number of children as their human capital rises over time because their higher level of human capital compensates for their lower fertility. In the long run, families with a higher education ability end up having a higher level of human capital, and all families choose the same steady-state fertility rate. However, high-ability families' evolutionary disadvantage in the short run implies that the population share of high-ability families decreases and the population share of low-ability families increases toward the steady-state distribution.

As a result, the population becomes less educated on average because the more educated parents have fewer children. This theoretical finding is consistent with the empirical evidence for a negative relationship between fertility and education.[3] Furthermore, our analysis suggests that this phenomenon is due to the evolutionary process continuing to operate behind the scenes in modern times,[4] which in turn stifles innovation and technological progress.

10.1   An Innovation-Driven Growth Model with Heterogeneous Agents

We introduce heterogeneous agents to the Romer model in the previous chapter. As before, we consider a simple structure of overlapping generations and human capital accumulation. Each agent lives for

---

[3]See, for example, Chu *et al.* (2024a).

[4]Galor and Moav (2002) also consider two types of agents and show that natural selection favors the quantity type and works against the quality type in the modern economy.

three periods. In youth, the agent accumulates human capital. In working age, the agent allocates time between work, fertility, and education of the next generation. In old age, the agent consumes the savings.

10.1.1 Heterogeneous agents

There are two types of families indexed by subscript $i \in \{L, H\}$.[5] Within each family i, the utility of an agent who works at time t is given by

$$u_{i,t} = (1 - \gamma) \ln c_{i,t+1} + \gamma \ln n_{i,t} + \kappa \ln h_{i,t+1}, \qquad (10.1)$$

where $c_{i,t+1}$ is the agent's consumption in old age, $n_{i,t}$ denotes the number of children the agent has, $\gamma \in (0, 1)$ is the fertility preference parameter, $h_{i,t+1}$ denotes the level of human capital that the agent passes onto each child, and $\kappa \geq 0$ is the education preference parameter. We assume that all agents within the same family i have the same level of human capital $h_{i,0}$ at time 0. Then, they will also have the same level of human capital $h_{i,t}$ for all t as an endogenous outcome.

The agent allocates $e_{i,t}$ units of time to the education of the next generation. We specify the following accumulation equation of human capital[6]:

$$h_{i,t+1} = \xi_i e_{i,t} + h_{i,t}, \qquad (10.2)$$

where the ability parameter $\xi_i > 0$ is heterogeneous across the two types of families such that $\xi_L < \xi_H$. The (unweighted) average

---

[5]Chu *et al.* (2024a) consider the general case with a continuum of heterogeneous types of families.

[6]For simplicity, we assume the human capital depreciation rate d to be zero in this chapter.

education ability of the two types of families is[7]

$$\bar{\xi} \equiv \frac{\xi_L + \xi_H}{2}.$$

We capture the heterogeneity across families by their differences in ξ_i, which in turn give rise to an endogenous distribution of human capital. Focusing on heterogeneity in ξ_i has the advantage of yielding a stationary population distribution in which both types of families coexist in the long run, whereas heterogeneity in other parameters, such as γ or κ, implies that only families with the largest γ or smallest κ would remain in the long run.

An agent in family i allocates $1 - e_{i,t} - \rho n_{i,t}$ units of time to work and earns $(1 - e_{i,t} - \rho n_{i,t})w_t h_{i,t}$ as real wage income, where the parameter $\rho \in (0,1)$ determines the time cost of fertility, as before. The agent devotes the entire wage income to saving at time t and consumes the return at time $t + 1$:

$$c_{i,t+1} = (1 + r_{t+1})(1 - e_{i,t} - \rho n_{i,t})\, w_t h_{i,t}, \qquad (10.3)$$

where r_{t+1} is the real interest rate. Substituting (10.2) and (10.3) into (10.1), the agent maximizes

$$\max_{e_{i,t}, n_{i,t}} u_{i,t} = (1 - \gamma) \ln\left[(1 + r_{t+1})(1 - e_{i,t} - \rho n_{i,t})\, w_t h_{i,t}\right]$$

$$+ \gamma \ln n_{i,t} + \kappa \ln(\xi_i e_{i,t} + h_{i,t}),$$

taking $\{r_{t+1}, w_t, h_{i,t}\}$ as given. The utility-maximizing level of fertility $n_{i,t}$ is

$$n_{i,t} = \frac{\gamma}{\rho(1 + \kappa)}\left(1 + \frac{h_{i,t}}{\xi_i}\right), \qquad (10.4)$$

which is decreasing in ξ_i but increasing in $h_{i,t}$. In other words, a family that is less capable of accumulating human capital or has a

---

[7]It is useful to note that $\bar{\xi}$ is the unweighted mean which is exogenous, whereas the weighted mean changes endogenously as the population share of families evolves over time.

higher level of human capital chooses to have more children. The utility-maximizing level of education $e_{i,t}$ is

$$e_{i,t} = \frac{\kappa}{1+\kappa}\left(1 - \frac{h_{i,t}}{\xi_i \kappa}\right), \tag{10.5}$$

which is increasing in ξ_i but decreasing in $h_{i,t}$. In summary, for a given $h_{i,t}$, a family that has a higher ability ξ_i chooses a higher level of education $e_{i,t}$ but a smaller number $n_{i,t}$ of children, reflecting the quality–quantity trade-off faced by different families.

10.1.2 Dynamics of human capital and population

Substituting (10.5) into (10.2) yields the autonomous and stable dynamics of human capital in family i as

$$h_{i,t+1} = \frac{\kappa}{1+\kappa}\left(\xi_i + h_{i,t}\right), \tag{10.6}$$

where $h_{i,t+1}$ is increasing in ξ_i and $h_{i,t}$. The total amount of human capital in the economy at time t is

$$H_t = h_{L,t}N_{L,t} + h_{H,t}N_{H,t} = \sum_{i \in \{L,H\}} h_{i,t}N_{i,t},$$

where $N_{i,t}$ is the (working-age) population size of family i. The law of motion for $N_{i,t}$ is

$$N_{i,t+1} = n_{i,t}N_{i,t} = \frac{\gamma}{\rho(1+\kappa)}\left(1 + \frac{h_{i,t}}{\xi_i}\right)N_{i,t},$$

and the population size in the economy at time t is

$$N_t = \sum_{i \in \{L,H\}} N_{i,t}.$$

Let's define $s_{i,t} \equiv N_{i,t}/N_t$ as the population share of family i. The population share $s_{i,t}$ of family i at time $t \geq 1$ is given by

$$s_{i,t} = \frac{\prod_{\tau=0}^{t-1} n_{i,\tau} N_{i,0}}{\sum_{i \in \{L,H\}} \prod_{\tau=0}^{t-1} n_{i,\tau} N_{i,0}}, \tag{10.7}$$

where we use (10.4) and (10.6) to obtain the fertility decision $n_{i,t}$ of family i at time t as

$$n_{i,t} = \frac{\gamma}{\rho(1+\kappa)} \left\{ \sum_{\tau=0}^{t-1} \left(\frac{\kappa}{1+\kappa}\right)^{\tau} + \left(\frac{\kappa}{1+\kappa}\right)^{t} \left(1 + \frac{h_{i,0}}{\xi_i}\right) \right\},$$

which is decreasing in ξ_i. From (10.7), we see that a lower fertility rate $n_{i,t}$ in any one period affects $s_{i,t}$ in all future generations. Therefore, if the high-ability families experience a temporary reproduction loss, then the economy would have a lower share of high-ability agents forever. As we will see, this evolutionary process would also permanently lower human capital, innovation, and economic growth.

10.1.3 Industrial output

This part of the model is the same as Section 9.1.3. The production function for final output Y_t (the numeraire) is given by (9.8). The conditional demand functions for human-capital-embodied production labor $H_{Y,t}$ and differentiated intermediate goods $X_t(j)$ are given by (9.9) and (9.10), respectively.

10.1.4 Intermediate goods

This part of the model is also the same as Section 9.1.4. The profit function for each intermediate good j is given by (9.11). The monopolistic firm maximizes profit subject to the demand function for $X_t(j)$ in (9.10) to derive the monopolistic price as $p_t(j) = 1/\varepsilon > 1$ in (9.12). Substituting $p_t(j) = 1/\varepsilon$ into (9.10) shows that $X_t(j) = X_t$ for all $j \in [0, A_t]$. Then, the equilibrium amount of monopolistic profit is given by (9.13).

10.1.5 Innovation

This part of the model is largely the same as Section 9.1.5. The value of a newly invented intermediate good at the end of time t is given by (9.14). New products are invented by R&D entrepreneurs, who employ $H_{R,t}$ units of human-capital-embodied labor. The innovation process is given by $\Delta A_t = \vartheta A_t H_{R,t}/N_t$ in (9.15). If the following free-entry condition holds:

$$\Delta A_t v_t = w_t H_{R,t} \Leftrightarrow \frac{\vartheta A_t v_t}{N_t} = w_t, \tag{10.8}$$

then R&D $H_{R,t}$ would be positive at time t. If $\vartheta A_t v_t/N_t < w_t$, then R&D does not take place at time t (i.e., $H_{R,t} = 0$). Similar to the previous chapter, it can be shown that R&D $H_{R,t}$ is positive at time t if and only if the following inequality holds:

$$\frac{1}{\vartheta} < \sum_{i \in \{L,H\}} (1 - e_{i,t} - \rho n_{i,t})\, h_{i,t} s_{i,t}. \tag{10.9}$$

10.1.6 Aggregation

Imposing symmetry on (9.8) yields $Y_t = H_{Y,t}^{1-\varepsilon} A_t X_t^{\varepsilon}$. Then, we substitute (9.10) and (9.12) into this equation to derive the same aggregate production function as before:

$$Y_t = \varepsilon^{2\varepsilon/(1-\varepsilon)} A_t H_{Y,t}. \tag{10.10}$$

Using $A_t X_t = \varepsilon^2 Y_t$, we obtain the following resource constraint on the final good:

$$\sum_{i \in \{L,H\}} c_{i,t} N_{i,t-1} = Y_t - A_t X_t = (1 - \varepsilon^2) Y_t, \tag{10.11}$$

where $\sum_{i \in \{L,H\}} c_{i,t} N_{i,t-1}$ is aggregate consumption by the old agents at time t. Finally, the resource constraint on human-capital-embodied labor is modified as

$$\sum_{i \in \{L,H\}} (1 - e_{i,t} - \rho n_{i,t})\, h_{i,t} N_{i,t} = H_{Y,t} + H_{R,t}. \tag{10.12}$$

10.2   Stages of Economic Development

As in the previous chapter, there are two stages of economic development. The first stage features only human capital accumulation. The second stage features both human capital accumulation and innovation. The endogenous transition from the first stage to the second stage with innovation-driven growth does not always occur.

10.2.1   Stage 1: Human capital accumulation only

The initial level of human capital for each agent in family i is $h_{i,0}$. Suppose the following inequality holds at time 0:

$$\frac{1}{\vartheta} > \sum_{i \in \{L,H\}} (1 - e_{i,0} - \rho n_{i,0})\, h_{i,0} s_{i,0}$$

$$= \frac{1-\gamma}{1+\kappa} \sum_{i \in \{L,H\}} \left(1 + \frac{h_{i,0}}{\xi_i}\right) h_{i,0} s_{i,0}, \qquad (10.13)$$

which uses (10.4) and (10.5). In (10.13), both the initial population share $s_{i,0} \equiv N_{i,0}/N_0$ and initial human capital $h_{i,0}$ are exogenously given. Then, (10.13) implies that $H_{R,0} = 0$ and

$$H_{Y,0} = \frac{1-\gamma}{1+\kappa} \sum_{i \in \{L,H\}} \left(1 + \frac{h_{i,0}}{\xi_i}\right) h_{i,0} N_{i,0}. \qquad (10.14)$$

In this stage of development, the economy features only human capital accumulation. Human capital $h_{i,t}$ accumulates according to the autonomous and stable dynamics in (10.6). However, as long as the following inequality holds at time t:

$$\frac{1}{\vartheta} > \sum_{i \in \{L,H\}} (1 - e_{i,t} - \rho n_{i,t})\, h_{i,t} s_{i,t}$$

$$= \frac{1-\gamma}{1+\kappa} \sum_{i \in \{L,H\}} \left(1 + \frac{h_{i,t}}{\xi_i}\right) h_{i,t} s_{i,t}, \qquad (10.15)$$

we continue to have $H_{R,t} = 0$ and

$$H_{Y,t} = \frac{1-\gamma}{1+\kappa} \sum_{i\in\{L,H\}} \left(1 + \frac{h_{i,t}}{\xi_i}\right) h_{i,t} N_{i,t}. \qquad (10.16)$$

Substituting (10.16) into (10.10) yields the level of industrial output per worker as

$$y_t \equiv \frac{Y_t}{N_t} = \varepsilon^{2\varepsilon/(1-\varepsilon)} A_0 \frac{H_{Y,t}}{N_t} = \varepsilon^{2\varepsilon/(1-\varepsilon)} A_0 \frac{1-\gamma}{1+\kappa}$$

$$\times \sum_{i\in\{L,H\}} \left(1 + \frac{h_{i,t}}{\xi_i}\right) h_{i,t} s_{i,t}, \qquad (10.17)$$

where A_0 remains at the initial level and industrial output increases as human capital accumulates.

10.2.2 Does innovation emerge?

Equation (10.6) shows that human capital $h_{i,t}$ converges to a steady state given by

$$h_i^* = \kappa \xi_i, \qquad (10.18)$$

which is increasing in family i's ability ξ_i. Substituting (10.18) into (10.4) and (10.5) yields the steady-state levels of education and fertility given by

$$e_i^* = e^* = 0, \qquad (10.19)$$

$$n_i^* = n^* = \frac{\gamma}{\rho}, \qquad (10.20)$$

respectively, which implies positive population growth $n^* > 1$ with $\gamma > \rho$ and negative population growth $n^* < 1$ with $\gamma < \rho$. Also, n^* is the same across all families because they are independent of ξ_i. In other words, the negative effect of ξ_i and the positive effect of h_i^* on n_i^* cancel each other. As a result, the distribution of the population share of different families is stationary in the long run. In this case, (10.9) implies that if the following inequality holds:

$$\frac{1}{\vartheta} < (1 - e^* - \rho n^*) \sum_{i \in \{L,H\}} h_i^* s_i^* = (1 - \gamma)\kappa \sum_{i \in \{L,H\}} \xi_i s_i^*, \quad (10.21)$$

where s_i^* is the steady-state population share of family i and can be obtained from (10.7) by taking the limit $t \to \infty$, then human capital accumulation eventually triggers the activation of innovation, under which the R&D condition in (10.8) holds and R&D $H_{R,t}$ becomes positive.

10.2.3   Stage 2: Innovation and human capital accumulation

We now derive the growth rate of y_t in the second stage. Substituting (10.10) into (9.9) yields the equilibrium wage rate as

$$w_t = (1 - \varepsilon)\varepsilon^{2\varepsilon/(1-\varepsilon)} A_t. \quad (10.22)$$

Then, substituting (10.22) into (10.8) yields the equilibrium invention value as

$$v_t = \frac{(1 - \varepsilon)\varepsilon^{2\varepsilon/(1-\varepsilon)}}{\vartheta} N_t. \quad (10.23)$$

The structure of overlapping generations implies that the value of assets at the end of time t must equal the amount of savings at time t, given by wage income at time t:

$$A_{t+1} v_t = w_t \sum_{i \in \{L,H\}} (1 - e_{i,t} - \rho n_{i,t}) h_{i,t} N_{i,t} = w_t(H_{Y,t} + H_{R,t}),$$

$$(10.24)$$

where the second equality uses (10.12). Substituting (10.22) and (10.23) into (10.24) yields

$$A_{t+1} = \frac{\vartheta A_t}{N_t}(H_{Y,t} + H_{R,t}). \quad (10.25)$$

Combining (9.15) and (10.25) yields the equilibrium level of $H_{Y,t}$ as

$$\frac{H_{Y,t}}{N_t} = \frac{1}{\vartheta} \tag{10.26}$$

for all t. Substituting (10.4), (10.5), and (10.26) into (10.12) yields the equilibrium level of $H_{R,t}$ as

$$\begin{aligned}
\frac{H_{R,t}}{N_t} &= \sum_{i\in\{L,H\}} (1 - e_{i,t} - \rho n_{i,t})\, h_{i,t} s_{i,t} - \frac{H_{Y,t}}{N_t} \\
&= \frac{1-\gamma}{1+\kappa} \sum_{i\in\{L,H\}} \left(1 + \frac{h_{i,t}}{\xi_i}\right) h_{i,t} s_{i,t} - \frac{1}{\vartheta}.
\end{aligned} \tag{10.27}$$

We can now substitute (10.27) into (9.15) to derive the equilibrium growth rate of A_t as

$$g_t \equiv \frac{\Delta A_t}{A_t} = \frac{\vartheta H_{R,t}}{N_t} = \vartheta \frac{1-\gamma}{1+\kappa} \sum_{i\in\{L,H\}} \left(1 + \frac{h_{i,t}}{\xi_i}\right) h_{i,t} s_{i,t} - 1, \tag{10.28}$$

which is also the equilibrium growth rate of output per worker, given by $y_t = \varepsilon^{2\varepsilon/(1-\varepsilon)} A_t/\vartheta$. Finally, the steady-state equilibrium growth rate of A_t and y_t is

$$g^* = \vartheta(1-\gamma)\kappa \sum_{i\in\{L,H\}} \xi_i s_i^* - 1, \tag{10.29}$$

where the steady-state population share s_i^* of family i depends on the initial distribution of $h_{i,0}$ and the exogenous value of ξ_i and can be obtained from (10.7) by taking the limit $t \to \infty$.

10.3 Evolution in the Modern Economy

Equation (10.13) shows that innovation occurs at time 0 if and only if the following inequality holds:

$$\frac{1-\gamma}{1+\kappa} \sum_{i\in\{L,H\}} \left(1 + \frac{h_{i,0}}{\xi_i}\right) h_{i,0} s_{i,0} > \frac{1}{\vartheta}. \tag{10.30}$$

Suppose we consider a useful benchmark of an equal initial population share $s_{i,0} = 1/2$ and an equal initial level of human capital $h_{i,0} =$

h_0 for all $i \in [0, 1]$. Then, the left-hand side of (10.30) simplifies to

$$\frac{1-\gamma}{1+\kappa} \left[1 + \frac{h_0}{2}\left(\frac{1}{\xi_L} + \frac{1}{\xi_H}\right)\right] h_0 > \frac{1-\gamma}{1+\kappa}\left(1 + \frac{h_0}{\bar{\xi}}\right) h_0, \qquad (10.31)$$

where $(1/\xi_L + 1/\xi_H)/2 > 1/\bar{\xi}$ due to Jensen's inequality. In other words, heterogeneity in ξ_i makes innovation more likely to occur at time 0 than the case without heterogeneity (i.e., $\xi_i = \bar{\xi}$ for $i \in \{L, H\}$). Due to heterogeneity, some agents supply more human capital for production and innovation, whereas others supply less. Equation (10.31) implies that the former effect dominates the latter effect such that the initial amount of human capital available for production and innovation is larger due to heterogeneity in ξ_i.

How does the population share $s_{i,t}$ evolve over time? Given the benchmark of an equal initial population share $s_{i,0} = 1/2$ and an equal initial level of human capital $h_{i,0} = h_0$ for all $i \in \{L, H\}$, the fertility of family i at time 0 is

$$n_{i,0} = \frac{\gamma}{\rho(1+\kappa)}\left(1 + \frac{h_0}{\xi_i}\right),$$

which is decreasing in ξ_i. For the high-ability families with $\xi_H > \xi_L$, their population growth rate $n_{H,0}$ would be lower than that of the low-ability families $n_{L,0}$. However, they will have a higher level of human capital in the next period:

$$h_{H,1} = \frac{\kappa}{1+\kappa}\left(\xi_H + h_0\right) > \frac{\kappa}{1+\kappa}\left(\xi_L + h_0\right) = h_{L,1}.$$

This higher level of human capital increases the fertility rate $n_{H,1}$ and reduces the difference between $n_{H,1}$ and $n_{L,1}$. However, $n_{H,t}$ remains lower than $n_{L,t}$ before $h_{H,t}$ converges to its steady-state level in (10.18), at which point the population growth rates of all families $i \in \{L, H\}$ converge to n^* in (10.20). Therefore, the population growth rates of families with ξ_H are lower than the population growth rates of families with ξ_L until $h_{H,t}$ converges to its steady-state level in (10.18). This temporary evolutionary disadvantage of high-ability agents will never be compensated for despite population trends being equal across families in the long run.

The above analysis implies that

$$\xi_L s_L^* + \xi_H s_H^* < \frac{\xi_L + \xi_H}{2} = \bar{\xi}$$

because $s_H^* < s_L^*$. Therefore, we also have the following inequality:

$$g^* = \vartheta(1-\gamma)\kappa\left(\xi_L s_L^* + \xi_H s_H^*\right) - 1 < \vartheta(1-\gamma)\kappa\bar{\xi} - 1, \qquad (10.32)$$

where $\vartheta(1-\gamma)\kappa\bar{\xi} - 1$ is the steady-state equilibrium growth rate under homogeneous families (i.e., $\xi_i = \bar{\xi}$ for all $i \in \{L, H\}$). In other words, the steady-state growth rate g^* becomes lower under heterogeneous families because the high-ability families' temporary evolutionary disadvantage reduces the average level of human capital and innovation in the long run.

Figure 10.1 plots the dynamics of the equilibrium growth rate of technology A_t and shows that heterogeneity can give rise to an earlier transition to innovation-driven growth but also leads to a lower long-run growth rate (relative to the case of homogeneous agents) due to the temporary evolutionary disadvantage of high-ability agents.

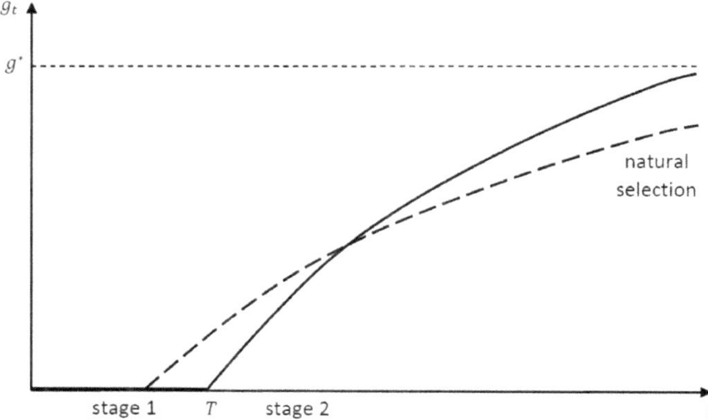

Figure 10.1. Dynamics of technology growth and impact of natural selection.

10.3.1 A more pessimistic scenario

In the previous section, a negative force of the evolutionary process exists but is not at its maximum level. In this section, we show that it is even possible for only the low-ability agents to remain in the population in the long run. Suppose we consider an alternative accumulation equation of human capital given by

$$h_{i,t+1} = \xi_i e_{i,t} + h_t, \tag{10.33}$$

where the accumulation of human capital in each family i depends on the average level of human capital in the population defined as

$$h_t \equiv \sum_{i \in \{L,H\}} s_{i,t} h_{i,t}.$$

Then, family i's utility-maximizing level of fertility is

$$n_{i,t} = \frac{\gamma}{\rho(1+\kappa)} \left(1 + \frac{h_t}{\xi_i} \right), \tag{10.34}$$

which shows that families with a lower ability ξ_i always have higher fertility $n_{i,t}$. Intuitively, the low-ability families benefit from the average level of human capital in the economy due to (10.33).

The utility-maximizing level of education $e_{i,t}$ is

$$e_{i,t} = \frac{\kappa}{1+\kappa} \left(1 - \frac{h_t}{\xi_i \kappa} \right), \tag{10.35}$$

which can be substituted into (10.33) to obtain the dynamics of human capital in family i as

$$h_{i,t+1} = \frac{\kappa}{1+\kappa} \left(\xi_i + h_t \right), \tag{10.36}$$

and the dynamics of the average level of human capital is then given by

$$h_{t+1} = \frac{\kappa}{1+\kappa} \left(\sum_{i \in \{L,H\}} s_{i,t} \xi_i + h_t \right). \tag{10.37}$$

The population growth rate of family i is given by

$$\frac{\Delta N_{i,t}}{N_{i,t}} = n_{i,t} - 1 = \frac{\gamma}{\rho(1+\kappa)}\left(1 + \frac{h_t}{\xi_i}\right) - 1, \qquad (10.38)$$

which is decreasing in the ability parameter ξ_i and depends on the average level of human capital h_t. Therefore, the families with lower ability ξ_L will dominate the population in the long run, and the high-ability families will disappear (i.e., $s_{H,t} \to 0$). Consequently, the average level of ability in the population converges to the lowest level, i.e.,

$$\sum_{i \in \{L,H\}} s_{i,t}\xi_i \to \xi_L. \qquad (10.39)$$

Due to this evolutionary process, the steady-state average level of human capital in the economy is given by

$$h^* = \kappa\xi_L. \qquad (10.40)$$

In the presence of innovation-driven growth, the steady-state equilibrium growth rate of A_t and y_t is

$$g^* = \vartheta(1-\gamma)\kappa\xi_L - 1, \qquad (10.41)$$

which is now determined by the *lowest* level of ability in the population. In this case, the evolutionary process works against technological progress and economic growth by selecting households with the lowest ability.

10.4   Summary and Discussion

In this chapter, we have introduced heterogeneous agents to the Romer model with endogenous fertility and human capital accumulation in order to explore how the evolutionary process affects innovation and technological progress in the modern economy. We consider the case in which households differ in their ability to accumulate human capital. Within this growth-theoretic framework, we obtain a *survival-of-the-weakest* scenario, which at first may seem contradictory to the hypothesis on "the survival of the fittest," made famous by Darwin (1869). However, our analysis shows that the survival of the fittest is the survival of the most fertile, which simply happens to be the low-ability households in the short run. In the long run, the high-ability households can accumulate enough human capital to overcome their temporary evolutionary disadvantage, which however has a lasting negative impact on innovation and technological progress.

In an alternative scenario, however, it is possible for the high-ability families to gradually fade out in the population, in which case only the low-ability families remain in the population in the long run. This process has detrimental effects on the economy by reducing human capital, innovation, and economic growth. Is there empirical evidence for these negative effects on education and innovation in the modern economy? Chu *et al.* (2024a) examine cross-country data and provide empirical evidence that heterogeneity in education ability indeed has adverse effects on education, innovation, and economic growth in the long run.

Afterword

In this book, we have developed a growth-theoretic framework to explore how archaic humans evolved into modern humans and how human society evolved from a hunting-gathering economy to an agricultural economy and eventually to a modern industrial economy with human capital formation and innovation. Our growth-theoretic analysis shows that all these evolutions are endogenous and only occur under certain conditions. Therefore, the journey of our ancestors over the past 2 million years was far from destined and could have turned out to be quite different. Under different conditions, another human species or multiple human species could have been the surviving humans, and the surviving humans could have remained in hunting-gathering tribes or agricultural settlements indefinitely. Even if an industrial economy had emerged, human capital could have remained at a sufficiently low level, under which innovation would not have taken place. In this case, the economy would not generate the kind of rapid growth in the standard of living that has been experienced by some countries in the past few centuries. The trajectory of humanity as we know it today became inevitable only after certain critical points in human history, which may be the survival of modern humans, the discovery of agriculture, the invention of the steam engine, or the emergence of modern innovation. Just imagine that for a moment.

Or imagine the quality of life of our species over the next 2 million years given the current technological progress. Perhaps, such an imagination is not necessary. As Harari (2015, p. 6) writes, "[i]t is doubtful whether *Homo sapiens* will still be around a thousand years from now, so 2 million years is really out of our league." Hopefully, what future technological progress brings to our future generations is the next stage of human evolution, rather than human extinction.

References

Aghion, P. and Howitt, P., 1992. A model of growth through creative destruction. *Econometrica*, 60, 323–351.

Ang, J., 2015. Agricultural transition and the adoption of primitive technology. *Economic Inquiry*, 53, 1818–1838.

Ashraf, Q. and Galor, O., 2011. Dynamics and stagnation in the Malthusian epoch. *American Economic Review*, 101, 2003–2041.

Ashraf, Q. and Galor, O., 2013. The "Out of Africa" hypothesis, human genetic diversity, and comparative economic development. *American Economic Review*, 103, 1–46.

Ashraf, Q., Galor, O., and Klemp, M., 2021. The ancient origins of the wealth of nations. *The Handbook of Historical Economics*, Chapter 22, 675–717.

Baker, M., 2008. A structural model of the transition to agriculture. *Journal of Economic Growth*, 13, 257–292.

Banks, W., d'Errico, F., Peterson, A.T., Kageyama, M., Sima, A., and Sanchez-Goni, M.-F., 2008. Neanderthal extinction by competitive exclusion. *PLoS One*, 3, e3972.

Barker, G., 2006. *The Agricultural Revolution in Prehistory: Why Did Foragers Become Farmers?* Oxford University Press.

Becker, G., Murphy, K., and Tamura, R., 1990. Human capital, fertility, and economic growth. *Journal of Political Economy*, 98, S12–S37.

Bello, D., 2020. Environmental change and Chinese empire. *Oxford Research Encyclopedia of Asian History*. Published online: 28 February 2020.

Boserup, E., 1965. *The Conditions of Agricultural Growth: The Economics of Agrarian Change under Population Pressure*. London: Allen & Unwin.

Bowles, S. and Choi, J.-K., 2019. The Neolithic agricultural revolution and the origins of private property. *Journal of Political Economy*, 127, 2186–2228.

Bricker, D. and Ibbitson, J., 2019. *Empty Planet: The Shock of Global Population Decline*. New York: Crown Publishing Group.

Chaudhry, A. and Garner, P., 2006. Political competition between countries and economic growth. *Review of Development Economics*, 10, 666–682.

Chu, A., 2010. Nation states vs. united empire: Effects of political competition on economic growth. *Public Choice*, 145, 181–195.

Chu, A., 2023. Natural selection and Neanderthal extinction in a Malthusian economy. *Journal of Population Economics*, 36, 1641–1656.

Chu, A., 2024a. Human brain evolution in a Malthusian economy. *Macroeconomic Dynamics*.

Chu, A., 2024b. A Malthusian model of hybridization in human evolution. MPRA Paper No. 121218.

Chu, A., Cozzi, G., Fan, H., and Hu, D., 2024a. Natural selection and innovation-driven growth. *Macroeconomic Dynamics*.

Chu, A., Cozzi, G., and Liao, C., 2013. Endogenous fertility and human capital in a Schumpeterian growth model. *Journal of Population Economics*, 26, 181–202.

Chu, A., Fan, H., and Wang, X., 2020a. Status-seeking culture and development of capitalism. *Journal of Economic Behavior and Organization*, 180, 275–290.

Chu, A., Furukawa, Y., and Wang, X., 2022a. Rent-seeking government and endogenous takeoff in a Schumpeterian economy. *Journal of Macroeconomics*, 72, 103399.

Chu, A., Furukawa, Y., and Zhu, D., 2016. Growth and parental preference for education in China. *Journal of Macroeconomics*, 49, 192–202.

Chu, A., Kou, Z., and Wang, X., 2020b. Effects of patents on the transition from stagnation to growth. *Journal of Population Economics*, 33, 395–411.

Chu, A., Kou, Z., and Wang, X., 2022b. Culture and stages of economic development. *Economics Letters*, 210, 110213.

Chu, A. and Peretto, P., 2023. Innovation and inequality from stagnation to growth. *European Economic Review*, 160, 104615.

Chu, A., Peretto, P., and Furukawa, Y., 2024b. Evolution from political fragmentation to a unified empire in a Malthusian economy. *Journal of Economic Behavior and Organization*, 222, 284–293.

Chu, A., Peretto, P., and Wang, X., 2022c. Agricultural revolution and industrialization. *Journal of Development Economics*, 158, 102887.

Chu, A., Peretto, P., and Xu, R., 2023. Export-led takeoff in a Schumpeterian economy. *Journal of International Economics*, 145, 103798.

Chu, A. and Xu, R., 2024. From Neolithic Revolution to industrialization. *Macroeconomic Dynamics*, 28, 699–717.

Cohen, M., 1977. *The Food Crises in Prehistory: Overpopulation and the Origins of Agriculture*. Yale University Press.

Cohen, M., and Armelagos, G., 1984. Paleopathology at the origins of agriculture. In M. Cohen and G. Armelagos (eds.) *Paleopathology at the Origins of Agriculture*. Orlando, FL: Academic Press, pp. 585–602.

Collins, J., Baer, B., and Weber, E. J., 2014. Economic growth and evolution: Parental preference for quality and quantity of offspring. *Macroeconomic Dynamics*, 18, 1773–1796.

Connolly, M., and Peretto, P., 2003. Industry and the family: Two engines of growth. *Journal of Economic Growth*, 8, 115–148.

Dalgaard, C.-J. and Strulik, H., 2015. The physiological foundations of the wealth of nations. *Journal of Economic Growth*, 20, 37–73.

Darwin, C., 1869. *On the Origin of Species by Means of Natural Selection, or the Preservation of Favoured Races in the Struggle for Life* (5th edition). London: John Murray.

Degioanni, A., Bonenfant, C., Cabut, S., and Condemi, S., 2019. Living on the edge: Was demographic weakness the cause of Neanderthal demise? *PLoS One*, 14, e0216742.

DeSilva, J.M., Traniello, J.F.A., Claxton, A.G., and Fannin, L.D., 2021. When and why did human brains decrease in size? A new change-point analysis and insights from brain evolution in ants. *Frontiers in Ecology and Evolution*, 9: 742639.

Diamond, J. 1997. *Guns, Germs, and Steel: The Fates of Human Societies*. New York: W.W. Norton.

Dixit, A., and Stiglitz, J., 1977. Monopolistic competition and optimum product diversity. *American Economic Review*, 67, 297–308.

Doepke, M., 2008. Growth takeoffs. In Steven N. Durlauf and Lawrence E. Blume (eds.) *The New Palgrave Dictionary of Economics* (2nd edition, pp. 1–7). London: Palgrave MacMillan.

Dow, G. and Reed, C., 2015. The origins of sedentism: Climate, population, and technology. *Journal of Economic Behavior & Organization*, 119, 56–71.

Dow, G. and Reed, C., 2022. *Economic Prehistory: Six Transitions That Shaped the World*. Cambridge University Press.

Dow, G., Reed, C., and Olewiler, N., 2009. Climate reversals and the transition to agriculture. *Journal of Economic Growth*, 14, 27–53.

Ehrlich, I. and Lui, F., 1997. The problem of population and growth: A review of the literature from Malthus to contemporary models of endogenous population and endogenous growth. *Journal of Economic Dynamics and Control*, 21, 205–242.

Eicher, T., 1996. Interaction between endogenous human capital and technological change. *Review of Economic Studies*, 63, 127–44.

Feng, X., Lu, D., Gao, F., Fang, Q., Feng, Y., Huang, X., Tan, C., Zhou, H., Li, Q., Zhang, C., Stringer, C., and Ni, X., 2024. The phylogenetic position of the Yunxian cranium elucidates the origin of Dragon Man and the Denisovans. bioRxiv preprint. https://doi.org/10.1101/2024.05.16.594603.

Fernandez-Villaverde, J., Koyama, M., Lin, Y., and Sng, T.-H., 2023. The fractured-land hypothesis. *Quarterly Journal of Economics*, 138, 1173–1231.

Fernihough, A., 2017. Human capital and the quantity-quality trade-off during the demographic transition. *Journal of Economic Growth*, 22, 35–65.

Fonseca-Azevedo, K. and Herculano-Houzel, S., 2012. Metabolic constraint imposes tradeoff between body size and number of brain neurons in human evolution. *Proceedings of the National Academy of Sciences*, 109, 18571–18576.

Funke, M. and Strulik, H., 2000. On endogenous growth with physical capital, human capital and product variety. *European Economic Review*, 44, 491–515.

Galor, O., 2005. From stagnation to growth: Unified growth theory. *Handbook of Economic Growth*, 1, 171–293.

Galor, O., 2011. *Unified Growth Theory*. Princeton University Press.

Galor, O., 2022. *The Journey of Humanity: The Origins of Wealth and Inequality*. Dutton.

Galor, O. and Klemp, M., 2019. Human genealogy reveals a selective advantage to moderate fecundity. *Nature Ecology & Evolution*, 3, 853–857.

Galor, O., Klemp, M., and Wainstock, D., 2024. Roots of cultural diversity. IZA Discussion Papers 17481.

Galor, O. and Michalopoulos, S., 2012. Evolution and the growth process: Natural selection of entrepreneurial traits. *Journal of Economic Theory*, 147, 759–780.

Galor, O. and Moav, O., 2002. Natural selection and the origin of economic growth. *Quarterly Journal of Economics*, 117, 1133–1191.

Galor, O. and Ozak, O., 2016. The agricultural origins of time preference. *American Economic Review*, 106, 3064–3103.

Galor, O. and Savitskiy, V., 2022. Climatic roots of loss aversion. Working Paper.

Gonzalez-Forero, M. and Gardner, A., 2018. Inference of ecological and social drivers of human brain-size evolution. *Nature*, 557, 554–557.

Grossman, G. and Helpman, E., 1991. Quality ladders in the theory of growth. *Review of Economic Studies*, 58, 43–61.

Growiec, J., 2006. Fertility choice and semi-endogenous growth: Where Becker meets Jones. *The B.E. Journals of Macroeconomics*, 6, 1–25.

Harari, Y. N., 2015. *Sapiens: A Brief History of Humankind*. New York: HarperCollins Publishers.

Harvati, K., Roding, C., Bosman, A.M., Karakostis, F.A., Grun, R., Stringer, C., Karkanas, P., Thompson, N.C., Koutoulidis, V., Moulopoulos, L.A., Gorgoulis, V.G., and Kouloukoussa, M., 2019. Apidima Cave fossils provide earliest evidence of *Homo sapiens* in Eurasia. *Nature*, 571, 500–504.

Heldstab, S.A., Isler, K., Graber, S.M., Schuppli, C., van Schaik, C.P., 2022. The economics of brain size evolution in vertebrates. *Current Biology*, 32, R697–R708.

Helpman, E., 2003. *General Purpose Technologies and Economic Growth*. The MIT Press.

Higham, T., Douka, K., Wood, R., Ramsey, C.B., Brock, F., Basell, L., Camps, M., Arrizabalaga, A., Baena, J., Barroso-Ruiz, C., Bergman, C., Boitard, C., Boscato, P., Caparros, M., Conard, N.J., Draily, C., Froment, A., Galvan, B., Gambassini, P., Garcia-Moreno, A., Grimaldi, S., Haesaerts, P., Holt, B., Iriarte-Chiapusso, M.J., Jelinek, A., Jorda Pardo, J.F., Maillo-Fernandez, J.M., Marom, A., Maroto, J., Menendez, M., Metz, L., Morin, E., Moroni, A., Negrino, F., Panagopoulou, E., Peresani, M., Pirson, S., de la Rasilla, M., Riel-Salvatore, J., Ronchitelli, A., Santamaria, D., Semal, P., Slimak, L., Soler, J., Soler, N., Villaluenga, A., Pinhasi, R., and Jacobi, R., 2014. The timing and spatiotemporal patterning of Neanderthal disappearance. *Nature*, 512, 306–309.

Hirshleifer, J., 1991. The paradox of power. *Economics and Politics*, 3, 177–200.

Hirshleifer, J., 2000. The macrotechnology of conflict. *Journal of Conflict Resolution*, 44, 773–792.

Horan, R., Bulte, E., and Shogren, J., 2005. How trade saved humanity from biological exclusion: An economic theory of Neanderthal extinction. *Journal of Economic Behavior & Organization*, 58, 1–29.

Hublin, J. J., Ben-Ncer, A., Bailey, S., Freidline, S., Neubauer, S., Skinner, M., Bergmann, I., Le Cabec, A., Benazzi, S., Harvati, K., and Gunz, P., 2017. New fossils from Jebel Irhoud, Morocco and the pan-African origin of Homo sapiens. *Nature*, 546, 289–292.

Iacopetta, M., 2010. Phases of economic development and the transitional dynamics of an innovation-education growth model. *European Economic Review*, 54, 317–330.

Iacopetta, M. and Peretto, P., 2021. Corporate governance and industrialization. *European Economic Review*, 135, 103718.

Jones, C., 1999. Growth: With or without scale effects. *American Economic Review*, 89, 139–144.

Jones, C., 2001. Was an industrial revolution inevitable? Economic growth over the very long run. *The B.E. Journal of Macroeconomics*, 1, 1–45.

Jones, C., 2003. Population and ideas: A theory of endogenous growth. In Aghion, P., Frydman, R., Stiglitz, J., and Woodford, M. (eds.) *Knowledge, Information, and Expectations in Modern Macroeconomics: In Honor of Edmund S. Phelps*. Princeton University Press.

Jones, C., 2019. Paul Romer: Ideas, nonrivalry, and endogenous growth. *Scandinavian Journal of Economics*, 121, 859–883.

Jones, C., 2022. The end of economic growth? Unintended consequences of a declining population. *American Economic Review*, 112, 3489–3527.

Kalemli-Ozcan, S., 2002. Does the mortality decline promote economic growth? *Journal of Economic Growth*, 7, 411–439.

Karayalcin, C., 2008. Divided we stand, united we fall: The Hume-North-Jones mechanism for the rise of Europe. *International Economic Review*, 49, 973–997.

Keskin, K., Ozgur, K., and Saglam, C., 2022. An individual-based network model explains Neanderthal extinction through competitive exclusion. *Journal of Economic Behavior & Organization*, 201, 163–175.

Kiser, E. and Cai, Y., 2003. War and bureaucratization in Qin China: Exploring an anomalous case. *American Sociological Review*, 68, 511–539.

Klemp, M. and Weisdorf, J., 2019. Fecundity, fertility and the formation of human capital. *Economic Journal*, 129, 925–960.

Krause, J., Fu, Q., Good, J. M., Viola, B., Shunkov, M. V., Derevianko, A.P., and Paabo, S., 2010. The complete mitochondrial DNA genome of an unknown hominin from southern Siberia. *Nature*, 464, 894–897.

Krugman, P., 1979. Increasing returns, monopolistic competition, and international trade. *Journal of International Economics*, 9, 469–479.

Lagerlof, N.-P., 2007. Long-run trends in human body mass. *Macroeconomic Dynamics*, 11, 367–387.

Lagerlof, N.-P., 2014. Population, technology and fragmentation: The European miracle revisited. *Journal of Development Economics*, 108, 87–105.

Laincz, C. and Peretto, P., 2006. Scale effects in endogenous growth theory: An error of aggregation not specification. *Journal of Economic Growth*, 11, 263–288.

Lin, J., 1995. The Needham puzzle: Why the Industrial Revolution did not originate in China. *Economic Development and Cultural Change*, 43, 269–292.

Liu, W., Martinon-Torres, M., Cai, Y.J., Xing, S., Tong, H.W., Pei, S.W., Sier, M.J., Wu, X.H., Edwards, R.L., Cheng, H., Li, Y.Y., Yang, X.X., de Castro J.M., and Wu, X.J., 2015. The earliest unequivocally modern humans in southern China. *Nature*, 526, 696–699.

Locay, L., 1989. From hunting and gathering to agriculture. *Economic Development and Cultural Change*, 37, 737–756.

Lopez, S., Van Dorp, L., and Hellenthal, G., 2015. Human dispersal out of Africa: A lasting debate. *Evolutionary Bioinformatics*, 11s2. 10.4137/EBO.S33489.

Lynn, R., 1990. The evolution of brain size and intelligence in man. *Human Evolution*, 5, 241–244.

Maddison, A., 2007. *Contours of the World Economy, 1-2030 AD: Essays in Macroeconomic History*. Oxford: Oxford University Press.

Malthus, T.R., 1798. *An Essay on the Principle of Population*. Oxford World's Classics.

Matranga, A., 2024. The ant and the grasshopper: Seasonality and the invention of agriculture. *Quarterly Journal of Economics*, 139, 1467–1504.

Murphy, K., Shleifer, A., and Vishny, R., 1989. Income distribution, market size and industrialization. *Quarterly Journal of Economics*, 104, 537–564.

Ni, X., Ji, Q., Wu, W., Shao, Q., Ji, Y., Zhang, C., Liang, L., Ge, J., Guo, Z., Li, J., Li, Q., Grun, R., and Stringer, C., 2021. Massive cranium from Harbin in northeastern China establishes a new Middle Pleistocene human lineage. *The Innovation*, 2, 100130.

North, D. and Thomas, R., 1973. *The Rise of the Western World: A New Economic History*. Cambridge University Press.

North, D. and Thomas, R., 1977. The first economic revolution. *Economic History Review*, 30, 229–241.

Nurkse, R., 1953. *Problems of Capital Formation in Underdeveloped Countries*. New York: Oxford University Press.

Ofek, H., 2001. *Second Nature: Economic Origins of Human Evolution*. Cambridge University Press.

Olsson, O., 2001. The rise of Neolithic agriculture. Working Paper in Economics No. 57, University of Goteborg.

Olsson, O. and Hibbs, D., 2005. Biogeography and long-run economic development. *European Economic Review*, 49, 909–938.

Peretto, P., 1999. Industrial development, technological change, and long-run growth. *Journal of Development Economics*, 59, 389–417.

Peretto, P., 2015. From Smith to Schumpeter: A theory of take-off and convergence to sustained growth. *European Economic Review*, 78, 1–26.

Peretto, P., 2021. Through scarcity to prosperity: Toward a theory of sustainable growth. *Journal of Monetary Economics*, 117, 243–257.

Price, M., 2020. Africans, too, carry Neanderthal genetic legacy: Ancient Europeans took Neanderthal DNA back to Africa. *Science*, 367, 497.

Prufer, K., de Filippo, C., Grote, S., Mafessoni, F., Korlevic, P., Hajdinjak, M., Vernot, B., Skov, L., Hsieh, P., Peyregne, S., Reher, D., Hopfe, C., Nagel, S., Maricic, T., Fu, Q., Theunert, C., Rogers, R., Skoglund, P., Chintalapati, M., Dannemann, M., Nelson, B.J., Key, F.M., Rudan, P., Kucan, Z., Gusic, I., Golovanova, L.V., Doronichev, V.B., Patterson, N., Reich, D., Eichler, E.E., Slatkin, M., Schierup, M.H., Andres, A.M., Kelso, J., Meyer, M., and Paabo, S., 2017. A high-coverage Neandertal genome from Vindija Cave in Croatia. *Science*, 358, 655–658.

Prufer, K., Racimo, F., Patterson, N., Jay, F., Sankararaman, S., Sawyer, S., Heinze, A., Renaud, G., Sudmant, P.H., de Filippo, C., Li, H., Mallick, S., Dannemann, M., Fu, Q., Kircher, M., Kuhlwilm, M., Lachmann, M., Meyer, M., Ongyerth, M., Siebauer, M., Theunert, C., Tandon, A., Moorjani, P., Pickrell, J., Mullikin, J.C., Vohr, S.H., Green, R.E., Hellmann, I., Johnson, P.L., Blanche, H., Cann, H., Kitzman, J.O., Shendure, J., Eichler, E.E., Lein, E.S., Bakken, T.E., Golovanova, L.V., Doronichev, V.B., Shunkov, M.V., Derevianko, A.P., Viola, B., Slatkin, M., Reich, D., Kelso, J., and Paabo, S., 2014. The complete genome sequence of a Neanderthal from the Altai Mountains. *Nature*, 505, 43–49.

Reardon, S., 2022. Did this gene give modern human brains their edge? *Nature*, 609, 665–666.

Reich, D., 2018. *Who We Are and How We Got Here: Ancient DNA and the New Science of the Human Past*. New York: Pantheon Books.

Richter, D., Grun, R., Joannes-Boyau, R., Steele, T., Amani, F., Rue, M., Fernandes, P., Raynal, J., Geraads, D., Ben-Ncer, A., and Hublin, J., 2017. The age of the hominin fossils from Jebel Irhoud, Morocco, and the origins of the middle stone age. *Nature*, 546, 293–296.

Romer, P., 1990. Endogenous technological progress. *Journal of Political Economy*, 98, S71–S102.

Schaefer, N. K., Shapiro, B., and Green, R. E., 2021. An ancestral recombination graph of human, Neanderthal, and Denisovan genomes. *Science Advances*, 7, eabc0776. DOI:10.1126/sciadv.abc0776.

Segerstrom, P., Anant, T., and Dinopoulos, E., 1990. A Schumpeterian model of the product life cycle. *American Economic Review*, 80, 1077–1091.

Smith, V., 1975. The primitive hunter culture, Pleistocene extinction, and the rise of agriculture. *Journal of Political Economy*, 83, 727–756.

Timmermann, A., 2020. Quantifying the potential causes of Neanderthal extinction: Abrupt climate change versus competition and interbreeding. *Quaternary Science Reviews*, 238, 106331.

Trinkaus, E., 1986. The Neandertals and modern human origins. *Annual Review of Anthropology*, 15, 193–218.

Trinkaus, E., 2011. Late Pleistocene adult mortality patterns and modern human establishment. *Proceedings of the National Academy of Sciences*, 108, 1267–1271.

van Valen, L., 1974. Brain size and intelligence in man. *American Journal of Biological Anthropology*, 40, 417–423.

Villmoare, B. and Grabowski, M., 2022. Did the transition to complex societies in the Holocene drive a reduction in brain size? A reassessment of the DeSilva *et al.* (2021) hypothesis. *Frontiers in Ecology and Evolution*, 10, 963568.

Weisdorf, J., 2005. From foraging to farming: Explaining the Neolithic Revolution. *Journal of Economic Surveys*, 19, 561–586.

Weisdorf, J., 2011. The Neolithic Revolution from a price-theoretic perspective. *Journal of Development Economics*, 96, 209–219.

Willmott, W. E., 1989. Dujiangyan: Irrigation and society in Sichuan, China. *Australian Journal of Chinese Affairs*, 22, 143–153.

Wood, B., 2011. Did early *Homo* migrate "out of" or "in to" Africa? *Proceedings of the National Academy of Sciences*, 108, 10375–10376.

Wood, B., and Collard, M., 1999. The human genus. *Science*, 284, 65–71.

Xia, H., Zhang, D., Wang, J., Fagernas, Z., Li, T., Li, Y., Yao, J., Lin, D., Troche, G., Smith, G.M., Chen, X., Cheng, T., Shen, X., Han, Y., Olsen, J.V., Shen, Z., Pei, Z., Hublin, J.J., Chen, F., and Welker, F., 2024. Middle and Late Pleistocene Denisovan subsistence at Baishiya Karst Cave. *Nature*, 632, 108–113.

Zeng, J., 1997. Physical and human capital accumulation, R&D and economic growth. *Southern Economic Journal*, 63, 1023–1038.

Zuo, X., Lu, H., Jiang, L., Zhang, J., Yang, X., Huan, X., He, K., Wang, C., and Wu, N., 2017. Dating rice remains through phytolith carbon-14 study reveals domestication at the beginning of the Holocene. *Proceedings of the National Academy of Sciences*, 114, 6486–6491.

Index

Q

Qin state, 68
quality–quantity trade-off, 111
quantitative spatial model, 67

R

resource competition, 32–35
Romer model, 97, 111–112, 125
rulers, 60–61

S

standard CES aggregator, 84
static model, 44–50, 73
steady-state equilibrium, 58, 65

steady-state population size, 24, 64
survival-of-the-weakest scenario,
 126

T

Thomas, R., 46

U

unified empire, 57–68
United States, 71

W

Weisdorf, J., 46
Western Europe, 71

www.ingramcontent.com/pod-product-compliance
Lightning Source LLC
Chambersburg PA
CBHW070751300925
32954CB00020B/182